George Elliott Casey

Money And Paper Currency

A Study for the Times

George Elliott Casey

Money And Paper Currency
A Study for the Times

ISBN/EAN: 9783744725736

Printed in Europe, USA, Canada, Australia, Japan

Cover: Foto ©Suzi / pixelio.de

More available books at **www.hansebooks.com**

MONEY

— AND —

PAPER CURRENCY,

A STUDY FOR THE TIMES.

— BY —

GEORGE E. CASEY, M. P.

OTTAWA :

PRINTED BY MACLEAN, ROGER & CO., WELLINGTON STREET.

1880.

PREFACE.

We cannot shut our eyes to the fact that a large section of the Canadian public are inclined to discuss the whole subject of currency *de novo*—to challenge existing systems, and to question propositions hitherto undoubted. Interest is added to the discussion by the fact that certain bank charters are about to expire, and by the proposal of the government to increase the circulation of Dominion notes. Under these circumstances, an addition to the literature of the question needs no apology for its appearance, though it can only become "current" by favor of the public.

I cannot pretend, at this time of day, to write anything both novel and sound on this subject. It has been my object to present a few leading principles and arguments in a convenient form, and to apply them to the solution of some problems now under discussion. It is unnecessary to consider all possible theories. When people see clearly that there is no mystery about currency, except such as has been created by those who claim to expound it, they will be able to judge new propositions, as they arise, by common sense reasoning from first principles.

The discussion of some of these "first principles" is embarrassing, from their very elementary character. They resemble Euclid's axioms in so far that they can only be proved by stating them. If a man does not admit at once that "the whole is greater than a part," no logic will convince him. The same is true of some elementary truths about currency. One can only explain their meaning—and may then be charged with repeating mere truisms. Yet, when the whole science of currency is attacked, one must go back to the beginning, and make sure that his axioms are sound.

The views and arguments advanced in this pamphlet are so far common property that I make no apology for inevitable plagiarisms. Yet I must acknowledge my special indebtedness to the concise and comprehensive manual of Prof. Bonamy Price, of Oxford, (" Currency and Banking "). It is hard to follow on the same route without stepping in his tracks. I have also quoted from a Review article by Sir John Lubbock, from Wilson ("Banking in England") and others. I acknowledge elsewhere what I have taken from Professor White of Cornell University.

OTTAWA, March, 1880.

TABLE OF CONTENTS.

—•◆•—

CHAPTER I.

WHAT IS MONEY?

It is not strange that men should be puzzled by obscure natural phenomena, or should fail to understand the nature of certain natural objects, or animal mechanisms. But it *is* amazing that men should lie under delusions in regard to the nature of a tool of their own invention—a tool, moreover, that is in every-day use, and has been so for ages. The uses and mode of operation of some complicated instruments are not obvious at first sight, but those whose duty it is to use such instruments generally know all about them : while others do not trouble themselves to theorize on the subject. A telephone is one of the newest inventions, and may be mysterious to those who have never studied it; but there is no dispute amongst electricians as to what it is or how it operates—there are no delusions about it amongst the ignorant. Those who ought to understand it do understand it thoroughly, while those who have had no opportunity of learning its nature do not profess to explain it. Yet, though money is nearly as old an invention as ploughs, and far more universally employed, and though there is nothing startling or mysterious about it at first sight, as there is about a telephone, there is nothing outside of religious dogma about which there are so many theories, delusions, and even superstitions. Surely this state of things must arise from mistaken methods of study, or from utter lack of study, on the part of those who ought to know the nature and uses of this instrument. Money has defined characteristics, both as a thing and as an instrument, and its nature and operation must be within the bounds of human knowledge, since it is a human invention to serve a certain purpose. Let us study it then scientifically as we would any other invention ; let us enquire what purpose it was intended to serve, and learn from history and observation how it performs its functions.

For what purpose, then, was money invented ?

Let us go back, in imagination, to the times before money was, and try to trace the wants which led to its introduction, and the way in which it meets those wants.

People then, as now, wanted many things they did not themselves produce, and such things they were of course compelled to buy. But their only means of buying was by the exchange of something they had, and could spare, for the thing they wanted—that is by *barter*. A farmer bought such wearing apparel as he could not make at home by giving grain, or wool, or cattle for it—a mechanic, by giving the products of his industry. But it often happened that what a man wanted was not to be had in exchange for the things he had to dispose of, or was only to be had at a place to which he could not conveniently take his own commodity. If a cooper wanted a pair of shoes, he might not be able to find a shoemaker who wanted a barrel. If the owner of a bullock wanted a coat, he might not be able to find a tailor who wanted a bullock. If a farmer wished to barter wheat for cloth, he might have to carry his wheat many miles to the cloth merchant—even if the latter were willing to take it. Under the above circumstances, the holder of a commodity which he could not barter directly for what he wanted had but one resource. He might be able to barter it for something else which the holder of the article he wanted would take in exchange therefor. Such a proceeding we call *double barter*. The shoemaker might say to the cooper : "I don't want a barrel, but I do want bacon; so, if you can find anyone to give you bacon for your barrel, you and I may make a bargain." This would at once involve the cooper in a troublesome search for a man who had bacon to spare and wanted a barrel, and he might not find him till his feet were frozen for want of shoes. The farmer, too, might spend a long time in getting his wheat exchanged for something more portable ; and, even then, might need to make a double barter at the end of his journey before he could effect his purchase of cloth. Land and buildings were of course, from their value and immovable nature, still harder to dispose of by barter for domestic supplies.

Besides all this inconvenience, there must have been great difficulty in fixing the relative values of the things exchanged. The cooper and the butcher might wrangle for

hours before they could agree how many pounds of bacon
were a barrel's-worth, and the same trouble would arise as
to the price of a pair of shoes in bacon. In fact, all such
barter could be nothing but an approximation to a fair exchange at best.

There was, then, a very real need of some article which
should serve as a third commodity in all double barters, and
consequently as a common measure of the value of the thing
sold, and of that ultimately obtained for it. There was as
great need of an instrument to measure and convey value, as
of a yard-stick or a cart to measure and convey commodities.

And nations, as they became civilized, were not long in
finding an instrument which served both purposes, and that
instrument is what we call *money*. They have all agreed on
one or more commodities which each individual might take
in exchange for what he had to sell, with the certainty that
he could barter it again at any time, and to any person, for
what he wanted to buy. Whoever had anything to sell exchanged it for this primitive money, and with this in turn
he made his purchases. It is easy to see how the use
of a constant third commodity, or medium of exchange in
double barters, afforded a measure of the value of other
commodities. The value of what was for sale was compared
with that of the commodity used as money, and expressed
in terms of the latter. It is clear, too, that the introduction
of this instrument did not change the nature of the transactions in which it was used. which were still, as before,
double barters. It only made such transactions always
possible, and much more convenient than formerly. It must
be noted also that money, the instrument of future purchases, was bought just as truly in each transaction as the
things for which it was, then and afterwards, exchanged.

It is important to notice what kind of commodities have
been used as money. Nothwithstanding their diversity,
they all posses certain characteristics in common. They have
been always either staple productions of the country in
which they were used, or staple commodities of its trade.
The oxen of legendary Greece and Rome, the pressed tea that
passed current in the trade with northern Asia, the furs of Hud-
son's Bay, the ivory of central Africa, are all suggestive of their
time and country. But the vital characteristic of them all—

the quality which made them fit for use as money—was· their value. It was only because their value was considerable for their bulk, well known, and fairly constant, that the seller could take them for his property, with the certainty that he could again barter them off without loss, and without inconvenience on the score of portability. Of course, even though they possessed these qualities, they would not have been current money without some sort of general agreement to take them—but without these qualities no such general agreement could have been brought about. No seller would take in payment a commodity which he thought was worth less than his own, or one which was likely to lose in value, or one of whose value others were likely to have a worse opinion than himself. *Value* and *agreement* are both requisite to make any commodity available as money ; but the first is a vital pre-requisite to the second.

These primitive forms of money remained commodities after their adoption as a medium of exchange, but when used in the latter capacity, they acquired the character of instuments besides—just as the wood and iron used in building a cart are commodities, although they constitute a carrying-tool when put together. An ox might have been bought for his meat, or to buy something else with—a tusk of ivory may be now bought in Africa to be used in the arts, or as money. In the one case either of these is a commodity only ; in the other it is still a commodity, but is also an instrument of exchange.

The work of this rude instrument was the same as that of the more perfect one we now use. It was *to circulate*, to go on buying and being bought, and so to facilitate the barter of what one man had to sell for what another had to dispose of. The qualities which made it useful as an instrument of exchange were its value and comparative portability—the most essential being its value. It bought with its value just as truly as an axe cuts with its edge, and was a buying tool just as truly as an axe is a chopping tool. It measured by its value as a yard stick does by its length, and was as truly a measuring tool as the latter.

We have now seen the purpose, nature, and mode of operation, of the earliest buying tools. Let us see further whether modern buying-tools resemble them in their main characteristics and uses, as modern axes resemble ancient ones. To do so we must trace the progressive steps of change and improvement in the invention.

These primitive monies were decidedly awkward in many ways· Some of the articles composing them were bulky and not portable. Hardly any were divisible into proportionate parts without loss or injury. Bullocks could walk of course, but not fast or far without hurt, and certainly were not adapted for pocket pieces. Ivory and furs are more valuable for their bulk, but still not very portable. Again, even in modern days, it is sometimes inconvenient to make a small purchase with a $20, note from scarcity of change. How much more awkward it must have been to buy a pair of shoes with an ox ? One could not cut off a roast in payment without decided injury to one's property. Calves might do for small change, but the shoemaker would not be likely to have a full supply. Furs are more manageable, but even with these one might be at a loss—unless one were a prairie Indian laying in a winter's supply of goods. It is evident then that though " Cattle-money," as these early expedients are sometimes generically termed, was a great assistance to trade, some better medium of exchange was required.

Nearly all civilized nations have thought that some of the metals met the requirements of the case more nearly than any other commodity. These are all of considerable value for their bulk, all the more or less easily divisible into proportionate parts, and all more or less fit to resist wear. We have noticed the impossibility of cutting up a *live* ox. It is hard to cut even a *dead* one into four quarters of equal value. It is impossible to cut up a bearskin or a buffalo hide without spoiling it. But one pound of any metal is worth just one-quarter as much as four pounds of that metal. And what is more, you can not only cut up a mass of metal without loss into pieces of proportionate value, but you can re-unite the pieces into a mass that is just as valuable as it was before you cut it. Gold, silver, and copper seem to posses in the highest degree those metallic characteristics which are useful for this purpose. They are very ductile, malleable, and divisible, and are not liable to rust or decay. These very qualities make them extremely useful in the arts, and therefore valuable. Gold and Silver, too, are by common consent of mankind—and especially of all womankind—desirable as personal ornaments. When we add that these three metals are all comparatively scarce and hard to obtain, it is easy to see how their great commercial value arose, which has earned for them the name of the "precious metals." Possessing thus great value for their bulk, and consequent portability, along with great divisibility and durability, it is no wonder that gold, silver, and copper should have been early, and almost universally, used as money. Iron, however, in some countries held the same relation to other metals that gold does in most, and was, in those, used for the same purpose. They circulated for a long time, in the form of ingots or bars—"Ingot money" as it is called. Now, though "Ingot money" was a great improvement on "Cattle money," yet the use of it was attended by some inconvenience. Like the *aes rude* of Rome, all kinds of ingot money were bought and sold by weight. The taker was compelled to test and weigh the ingots, and cut them if necessary. In fact it was scarcely possible to conclude a transaction without reference to a chemist, mechanic, or money-changer. Gradually means were contrived to avoid this trouble. In some communities, the stamp of a well-known dealer on an ingot was taken by most as a sufficient evidence of weight and purity. In others, nothing further was done than to mould the metal into pieces approximalety uniform in weight and shape—bricks, rings, and the like.

According to our present knowledge it is to the Greek race that we owe the next immense step in advance—the introduction of coinage. The earliest Greek coins were made either by the Lydians or Aeginetans—probably about 700 B.C. to 650 B.C. They were only rudely shaped pieces of metal, stamped with their weight and value, but they possessed all the vital characteristics of a true coinage. And what were these? Simply the authoritative ascertainment, and official declaration by the stamp they bore, of their weight and purity. Aristotle thus briefly and clearly states the origin of coins. "It became necessary, therefore, to think of certain commodities easily manageable, and safely transportable, and of which the uses are so general and so numerous that they insured the certainty of obtaining for them the articles wanted in exchange. The metals, particularly iron and silver and several others, exactly correspond to this description. They were employed therefore, by general agreement, as the ordinary standard of value and the common measure of exchange, being themselves estimated at first by bulk and weight, *and afterwards stamped in order to save the trouble of measuring and weighing them.*"

Did this metallic coin differ in any essential respect from the "Cattle money" and "Ingot money" which it superseded? We cannot see that it did. It was still a commodity, and its use as a tool of exchange still depended on its qualities and value as a commodity. The piece of gold after it was stamped was worth no more than before—except perhaps to the extent of the cost of that operation. The stamp added nothing to it, and took nothing from it. It only "saved," as Aristotle justly says, "the trouble of measuring and weighing it." And what was true of that coinage is true of all coinage. The value is in the metal— the stamp does not create it, but only certifies to it. If a hundred new gold dollars be melted into an ingot, the ingot will be worth one hundred dollars. If you take twenty ounces of gold to the English mint, you will get for it twenty ounces of sovereigns. The cost of minting is paid *by* the nation for the sake of the convenience *to* the nation. In fact Burns' well known couplet :

> " The rank is but the guinea-stamp,
> The man's the gold for a' that,"

is equally true when reversed. The " guinea-stamp " is but the patent of rank—the " gold " is the same sterling metal before it is ennobled as after. Of course a government may palm off base metal upon its confiding subjects by means of a lying mint mark, and thus invest it with an unreal value —till the fraud is discovered. And so may a grocer palm off adulterated sugar—till he is found out. But such frauds and forgeries cannot be taken to prove that the government stamp, or the grocer's assurances, add anything to the commercial value of pinchbeck gold or sanded sugar.

The fact that Kings and Governments have generally retained the right of coinage for themselves has given rise to some notion that it is theirs by "prerogative," and that this " prerogative " adds some special virtue to the operation. The real reason why Governments do, and should, retain the right to coin money is obvious. It is because no private party could do it so well, or give such authority to his certificates, as the nation—and because it is right that the nation should bear the cost of providing a great public convenience. It is a fact worth noticing, however, that the Roman State did allow certain great families to make and issue coin—under State supervision—for whose genuiness they were held responsible. Clearly the Romans did not think the prerogative added anything to the value of the metals coined.

It is interesting to notice the derivation of our words relating to coin. *Pecunia* (cattle) the older Latin word for money —whence our "pecuniary"—alludes both to the early Cattle-money and to the stamp on the first ·coins. *Moneta* again —our word " money "—is from the temple of *Juno Moneta* where the mint was situated.

We are now in a position to determine to what thing the word money is properly applicable, and what are the nature and uses of that thing. "Money," then, properly means metallic coin, but is also applied to certain other commodities formerly used for the same purpose as coin. All money is a commodity, used as a measure of value and a medium of exchange, for the purpose of facilitating barter. It is a measuring and buying tool, and it measures and buys in virtue of a certain quality,—namely, its commercial value— which is inherent in itself, and does not depend on the stamp it bears, but on its relation as a commodity to other commodities. Money is bought as really as it buys in every transaction in which it is used.

This is the answer which a scientific and historical survey of the subject enables us to give to the question at the head of this chapter.

GENERAL NOTES ON MONEY.

There are some other questions which we can now answer and which should be answered before we proceed further.

Is money wealth in any special sense ?

Certainly it is wealth, in the same sense that any other merchantable commodity is—but in no other. A man who holds one hundred dollars worth of wheat has as much wealth as one who has one hundred gold dollars—that is he has as much purchasing power. He can turn his wheat into dollars at any moment, and these again into whatever he requires. A man who inherits two thousand dollars in cash is no wealthier than he who inherits fifty acres of land, worth $40 per acre. How then has coined money come to be regarded as the essence, or highest embodiment, of wealth? Because it is one of the most condensed and effective forms of wealth, one of the forms in which it is most striking to the senses, and the one in which it is most easily used as a purchasing power. It is wealth in motion and in action, displaying publicly its wonderful forces. The possessor of lands or goods may have no realizing sense of his riches till he has turned them into cash. Then he immediately feels his being enlarged. He has "money in his pocket," and he feels a thrill of power. He has roused the sleeping giant who is his slave, and he rejoices in the exercise of his gigantic strength. He says to himself "This is indeed wealth; all my energies henceforth shall be devoted to obtaining *money.*"

The delusion is further heightened by the loose application of the word money to what is only money's-worth. We say "he makes money"—"he is worth untold money"—"he will leave a pot of money"—when we only mean wealth or property. The use of this figure of speech arises from the popular idea of money already referred to, and both the idea and the colloquial usage mutually strengthen each other.

It is quite another thing to ask whether wealth in the form of money is more desirable than other wealth. There are many circumstances in which it is, because it is so merchantable, convenient to keep, and steady in value. But it is to be remembered that the holder of money must forego the use he might otherwise make of that much wealth. He cannot keep money and use it, any more than he can eat his cake and have it. We shall consider this more fully when we come to treat of "capital."

What is a dollar?

A dollar is, by law, when dollars are coined or used as money, a piece of gold of a certain weight and

fineness, bearing the mint-mark which certifies to its
weight and purity. It is used as a measure of value by com-
paring it with other commodities. We say of any article that
it is "worth so many dollars"—which means that it will
buy so many, or that so many will buy it. In this way we
can compare the relative values of commodities by stating
the number of dollars to which they are equal. The word
"dollar" is also used in accounts to signify either a dollar or
some value equal to that of a dollar. We shall speak of so-
called "paper dollars" under another heading.

What is price?

The word "price," as used in commerce, means the
value of a commodity expressed by the number of dollars,
pounds, &c., as the case may be that it is worth. But
it is also true that the price of a commodity may
be expressed in any other commodity. The price of a hat
may be $5.—or it may be a pair of boots. But prices are
usually, for convenience, expressed in money.

What is the price of the commodity called a dollar?

Just whatever can be had in exchange for it. It may
be a bushel of wheat, or an axe, or an one-fifth interest
in a sheep, or an one-hundredth interest in a horse.
It changes from day to day with the changing commercial value of things the dollar is compared with.
While its price is thus going up and down, in reality.
in comparison with other things, it is customary—from its
use as a standard of value and the expression of price in dollars—to regard dollars or money as a sort of polar star, around
which all prices and values revolve, while itself remains im-
mutably fixed. It *is* so by a figure of speech, and we seldom
realize that when we quote the price of any commodity in
dollars, we are at the same time quoting the price of dollars
in that commodity. Yet when we say "the price of wheat
is $1.50 a bushel," we also state by implication that "the
price of a dollar in wheat is 40 lbs." Naturally, from un-
thinking use, has grown up the idea that "a dollar" is the expression of a certain value. But we have seen that it is not—
that it is only the name of a certain coin. The name of that coin
could convey no idea of value whatever, unless we mentally
compared it with something else—calculated in fact what
it would buy at the moment, or what it would cost to obtain

it. In this way it does of course convey an idea of value ; but one which varies with all conditions of general prices, and with the circumstances of the individual concerned. To the farmer it may suggest a bushel of wheat, or a new axe ; to the laborer a days work, or so many pounds of flour ; to the merchant the profit on a certain amount of capital, or so much of his clerk's time.

How much money does a community need ?

We have seen that money is a tool of exchange. It follows that the amount needed depends on the number of exchanges in which such a tool is required, just as the number of axes needed depends on the amount of chopping to be done. We shall consider, further, on what conditions of society, and what lines of trade, require most money in proportion to the business done. But no more definite answer than this can be given to our question. A community needs just as much money as must be used for the convenient transaction of its buying and selling. How much this is can only be determined by actual trial. If the business of a community goes on easily without anybody being compelled to resort to barter or other clumsy expedients, or to abstain from the exchange of commodities for want of money, that community has money enough for its wants. It may have much wealth, or be in a condition of national bankruptcy ; but it has as much money as is needed for the exchanges it is making.

The existence in a community of more money than it needs for the purpose of exchange is evidently a dead loss to the people. For, since money is a commodity that can only be obtained for value, and since the surplus over the needs of commerce is a tool for which there is no work, it is clear that such a state of things means the locking up of wealth in an unproductive form. It is as bad an investment as the purchase of threshing machines which must lie idle for want of work. It is of course easy to get rid of this surplus by exchanging it for other commodities a broad, and that is what is really done when a community is troubled with a "glut of gold."

How is the supply of money kept up?

Simply by the demand for it in the market, which causes new money to be made and offered for sale.

One deduction from the history of money should be specially noted. It is that all trade, whether carried on by means of money or not, is only a protracted or complicated barter. One buys money only to buy something else with the money, and so in the long run all trade transactions resolve themselves into the barter of one commodity, for some other commodity, no matter how many exchanges for money have come between. It is consequently no test of the profits of a man's business to note how much cash he may have on hand at the end of the year, as cash is only one form of wealth—one kind of commodity. He may have little cash but large profits in some other form, or he may have a large amount of cash, the proceeds of forced sales at ruinous rates. Neither has the amount of cash he pays or receives in dealing with a particular person any bearing on his prosperity. The same is true of nations. And yet there are those who assume that a nation's profits and prosperity can only be judged by the proportion of the proceeds of her annual sales that comes to her in cash at the year's end ! There are those who call themselves "authorities," and teach that the influx or efflux of the precious metals constitutes a nation's wealth or poverty ! But this by the way, as we are not studying political economy at large.

CHAPTER II.

PAPER CURRENCY.

We have now learned enough of the nature and uses of money proper, or metallic coin, to proceed intelligently with the study of certain substitutes for it, which are not money in themselves, but serve the same purpose as mediums of exchange. All such substitutes are termed generically " currency." The word bears its meaning on its face. It is from the latin *curro* (I run) and the characteristic of the thing signified is that it runs or circulates. Whatever passes freely without hitch or objection as a medium of exchange is a currency. Of course it will be seen that this definition includes money. But it also includes many other things which, from their use, are often confounded with money, bank notes being the most familiar to us—and is generally applied to these when spoken of as distinct from money.

Even in very rude times, tokens denoting the ownership of portions of property were used as currency instead of the actual commodities. Among the Russians, pieces cut out of skins were used for this purpose. They served both as samples, and titles to the skins, since the holder of the pieces claimed from the original owner those skins into which they fitted, But the typical currency—as distinct from money —consists of documents transferring the ownership of money. Indeed, for all practical purposes, we may say that *all* the currencies we know of consist of acknowledgements of debt payable in money.

Some documents of this kind, which pass current in limited circles, may prove useful as illustrations. We all know that promissory notes, bills of exchange, and drafts made by responsible parties, pass current to a great extent among business men instead of the actual cash they acknowledge to be due. Indeed most of our international transactions are settled by such means. Canadian exports to England are ultimately paid for by bills due from Canadian importers to parties in England, and the cash is ultimately collected from the makers of such bills. The object of this proceeding is obviously to save the expense and risk of bringing over specie. The reason why the Canadian exporter, or Canadian bank, is willing to take a particular bill, is that he believes the maker to be solvent and willing to meet his obligations. Documents of the nature of bills of exchange, though calling for certain weights of metal instead of for coined money, are still in existence, made (on baked clay) in Babylon more than 2,500 years ago, and appear to have been used in the same way, as modern ones. This sort of limited currency may in fact be taken to include all negotiable securities, notes, bonds, English consols, mortgages, the shares of corporations and the like. The conditions on which it is current are, that it shall acknowledge a debt, and that the debtor be one who is generally considered " good." We shall find that the same conditions affect the more general currency which we are about to notice.

CONVERTIBLE BANK-NOTES.

We owe to China the invention of the first true bank notes as we do so many other inventions. They first appeared in that country about 800 A.D. and were called " flying money." At a later date some sixteen prominent firms, united to form a bank of issue. There notes were issued in several series, each payable in three years from the date of issue. The Japanese also used paper money at one time, but never brought it to perfection and finally gave it up. A detailed history of bank notes would be as cumbrous as a full account of all coins. We must be content therefore with generalities, and pass on at once to modern bank notes as we know them in Europe and here. These are all, like the Chinese issues, promises to pay money, but differ from the latter in being payable on demand instead of at a fixed time.

Now the very terms of bank notes, which promise to pay money, show that they are not themselves money. How then do they serve the purpose of money, and why are they so often confounded with the latter both in common language and in the popular mind?

They serve the purpose of money just in the same way that deeds of land might. We have seen that money purchases by its value. So would land, and, as a deed is a transfer of land, the deed is all that need pass from hand to hand in a transaction. So, as bank notes are transfers of the ownership of money, acknowledged to be due by their makers, the handing over of the notes is as good as the handing over of the money. It is as good on one condition—namely that the issuer of the notes be honest, and able to pay the money they call for on demand. That is, bank notes depend for their value or purchasing power, altogether on the fact that they are convertible into money at the will of the holder. As soon as any suspicion arises, that the notes of any bank are not so convertible, they immediately fall in value. If the bank fail utterly to meet its notes, they become completely worthless. Between the two points of perfect confidence and worthlessness they may have a wide range of value, according to the general opinion of the probability of their redemption, and of the time when they will be redeemed. It is plain then that bank notes are subject to just the same

vicissitudes in value as promissory notes of private individuals, or other negotiable securities, and rest on just the same
basis as the latter—namely the credit of those who issue
them.

Bank Notes get into circulation by being paid out by the
bank for value, or for obligations to an equal amount given
to it by the taker of the notes. In the first case their issue is
equivalent to a loan made by the taker to the bank,for which
he takes the bank's acknowledgement of debt, knowing that
others will also be willing to accept the bank as *their* debtor
by taking its notes In the second case, the bank virtually
says to the man who asks a loan of capital—" We prefer to
lend you our notes instead of money--that is we will
lend you our *credit*, which is more generally acknowledged
than your own." And the borrower takes the the notes for
the reasons above mentioned. So a bank's issue of notes is
always considered one of its liabilities—and not an asset, as
it would be if notes were really money.

This argument may seem to many like an attempt to
prove an axiom, but it is a fact that in popular estimation
bank notes bear to a great extent the reputation of being
money. It is not wonderful that they do, especially in
America where their use is so much more common than that
of gold. The taker of bank notes finds that they buy just
as much as an equal nominal value of gold or other money,
and he is apt to conclude that things which produce the
same effect are identical. Yet, in order to any rational consideration of currency questions, we must remember that
bank notes are not money, any more than a deed is so much
land, or a warehouse receipt so much grain.

It is an important fact in connection with this species of
currency, that the amount of it in circulation cannot remain
permanently, or even long, in excess of the public demand
for bank notes. Whenever, from any cause, it exceeds that
demand, it is sure to be returned to the banks and converted
into gold, or into other obligations from the banks in the
form of credit on the books. Where more than one bank
issues notes, the proportion returned may not be equally
divided ; but the sum total of the circulation will be reduced
by the amount of the over-issue. An excess of bank notes is
an evil for the same reasons that an excess of gold is, and is
just as easily curable.

Before noticing national paper currency it will be necessary to explain the nature of laws declaring that any currency is "legal tender."

Every community, in which contracts to pay certain sums or to furnish certain commodities can be legally enforced, must have laws declaring what will be considered a proper fulfilment of such contracts, and what certain terms used therein shall be taken to mean. So we have laws declaring that the word "acre" in a contract shall mean a certain quantity of land—the word "bushel" a certain quantity of grain—the word "gallon" a certain quantity of liquid. In regard to money the law does just the same thing. It says that in contracts calling for money the word "dollar" shall mean a certain weight of gold, or a certain promise to pay such a piece of gold as the case may be, and that the offer of such pieces or promises to the amount named in the contract, and of these only, shall be a "legal tender" of payment. We have seen that by law under a contract calling for bushels, only certain weights of grain shall be legal tender. So the legal tender law, like that of weights and measures, simply settles the nomenculature of things, to avoid disputes in the settlement of contracts. It is evident that such a law can add no more to the value of the commodity called money than the law which fixes the number of pounds in a bushel does to the value of wheat. It simply settles what sort of a commmodity shall be money, and fixes the terminology of money. The same is true in regard to convertible notes of all kinds, since their value depends directly on that of money, to which they bear the same relation as warehouse receipts do to wheat. If any proof were needed we have it in the fact that Dominion Notes which *are* legal tender, and those of good banks which are *not* legal tender, circulate together at the same value. The effect of such laws on inconvertible notes will be considered in the proper connection.

NATIONAL PAPER CONVERTIBLE CURRENCY.

Governments have issued, and now issue, two forms of paper currency—convertible and inconvertible. The former consists of notes payable on demand in gold, like those of banks. The latter consists of notes payable, not on demand, but at some indefinite time—practically whenever the government sees fit to "resume specie payments." Both kinds are paid out by government to its creditors instead of money, and their issue is equivalent to effecting a forced loan without interest. The difference is that in the first instance the loan is recoverable at the will of the taker, or creditor, while, in the other, it is recoverable only at the will of the issuer, or debtor.

The characteristics of national demand-notes are so obviously similar to those of bank notes that they require but brief notice. They depend for general acceptance on the credit of the nation, as those of a bank depend on the credit of the bank ; and any suspicions of the solvency or good faith of the government would affect their value, just as similar suspicions would affect the value of bank notes. The extent of their circulation is also regulated in the same way as with bank notes, since any surplus is readily convertible into gold, and sure to be so converted.

NATIONAL INCONVERTIBLE PAPER CURRENCY.

We have already pointed out that though inconvertible notes acknowledge a debt, they fix no time for the payment of it. To carry out an illustration already used, we may say that while convertible notes resemble warehouse receipts for grain deliverable on demand—which grain, or the means of procuring it when called for, is believed to exist—inconvertible notes resemble warehouse receipts for grain whose existence is not guaranteed, and which is deliverable at the pleasure of the warehouseman. Now, we all know that a bank note payable, like the Chinese currency, in three years from date would not be taken as willingly as one payable on demand. The risk of the continued existence and solvency of the bank at the time named would be considerable—not to mention the inconvience to those who might need coin before that date. A bank note which only contained such an indefinite obligation as that of a greenback would be still less acceptable ; in fact, it would not circulate at all if anything more substantial could be had. Why, then, do national notes

2

of that description circulate? A nation has a great advantage in credit over any bank—at least, amongst its own citizens. Inconvertible notes pledge that credit to payment at some date, however remote, and citizens who believed in the honesty of their government would be apt to attach *some* value to the most indefinite national obligation. But it is doubtful whether, in an open market, such notes woul dever become current to such an extent as to be useful as a medium of exchange. Consequently, governments who issue them always declare them to be "legal tender." That is, they say to their creditors : "If you don't take these notes you may go unpaid ; but if you do take them, we shall authorize you to say to your own creditors what we now say to you." Of course, under such a provision of law they get at once into circulation, and, being inconvertible, when once out they stay in circulation.

But at what value will they be taken by the public generally ? Of course, under all contracts made previous to their issue they must be accepted at their face value, unless some legal provision be made excepting such contracts. After that, they must still be taken for as many dollars as they bear on their face ; *but will a dollar buy as much as formerly?* We have seen that the law which makes them legal tender has simply effected a change in the nomenclature of accounts. The word "dollar" will now mean, not a certain weight of gold, but a certain national obligation to pay that weight of gold at some indefinite time. Will the new dollar be worth as much as the old one? How shall we be able to determine whether it is or not ? By the comparative number of dollars that sellers are willing to take for their commodities—by the quantity of gold for example which one of the new dollars will buy. For, after such a change in nomenclature, gold dollars, which were formerly the standard of price, become mere commodities, and we have the apparent anomaly of a price *in* dollars *for* dollars. We have noticed that the value of gold dollars could only be ascertained by how much they would buy—their price in other commodities. The same is true of paper dollars—and as gold is the steadiest of commodities, and the world's standard's of price, the value of inconvertible notes is most correctly ascertained by their price in gold—or by the price of gold in such notes, which is the same statement in another form. If a paper dollar will buy a gold dollar, then the paper currency is as good as the gold currency. If it will not, then the paper currency is said to have depreciated—that is, it is less valuable dollar for dollar than the other. When this occurs the depreciation is expressed in different ways. In some countries the opinion of the world is taken as the standard, and in such the paper currency is spoken of as being at so much per cent discount —worth so many cents on the dollar for example. In others, as in the United States, the new currency is taken as the standard and gold is spoken of as having risen—being at a premium of so much per cent—each dollar worth a dollar and so many cents in paper.

Now, let us look at this question of value in the light of probability and experience. Apart from their character as legal tender, on what does the value of inconvertible notes depend ? Simply on the public estimate of the chances of ultimate payment, and of the time it may take place. Of course the former factor is the more important, since people might be willing to wait long for payment from a creditor known to be good. Yet, any deferred debt—still more, one deferred indefinitely — must lose in value somewhat from its very postponement. When that postponement involves a risk of ultimate loss, the decrease will be greater. Now it does involve that risk in the case of most inconvertible paper. The issue of such a currency is usually the last resort of a government sorely pinched for funds, through war costs or extravagance. It is a forced loan, exacted by a government whose credit is not good enough to allow it to borrow in any other way—which dare not even risk the issue of demand notes, for fear of inability to pay the proportion of them that might be presented. The future ability, or willingness to pay, of a government in such circumstances is always problematical, and there have been sufficient instances of repudiation to cause distrust. Patriotism and hopefulness on the part of its own citizens will always add to the value of such currency in their eyes ; but such feelings will not increase the value of it abroad. Under the best circumstances, the probability of payment at all, and its date, depend entirely on the honesty of the rulers. All sorts of political considerations may urge them to repudiation, or indefinite postponement—not to speak of baser temptations to which all men are subject, and which are especially rife in times of inflation. Moreover, we have seen that currency is a tool for which there is a certain amount of work in a community, namely, the facilitating of cash tran-- sactions, and that an over-supply of this tool, as of any other, will cause a fall in its value. Now, since "greenbacks"— for so we may conveniently call all paper of this kind— are inconvertible and must continue to circulate, and since the government must continue to issue for further expenses,. it is clear that an inconvertible currency, if its issue be con- tinued, inevitably involves an excess of circulation— unless the wants of commerce should increase as rapidly as the volume of currency, which is very unlikely. Now, if at its first issue it was weighted by so many doubts as to its ultimate goodness and speedy con-- vertibility, what will become of its value when such a dubious instrument of exchange is forced on the public largely in excess of their requirements ? Perhaps no better illustration can be found of the operation of both causes of weatness combined than in the currency of the late Con- federate States of America. It was said of this, with but slight exaggeration, that you took your money to market in a wheelbarrow, and brought back your purchases in your waistcoat pocket ! That of the United States, on the other hand, was at the worst of times a real ond valuable security. The nation was always strong, and reputed honest enough to pay sometime. Yet we all remember the time when a dollar in gold or Canadian currency would buy three dollars in greenbacks.

But, before quoting further instances, we must consider whether the law of legal tender has any effect on the value of that inconvertible " money " which it can undoubtedly make current. We have seen that it has no such effect in regard to gold or convertible notes. It simply makes them currency—embodies the agreement of the community that they shall be used for that purpose—but it does not, and cannot, fix the purchasing power of any such coin or note. And there is no ascertainable reason why it should have any effect on inconvertible notes. True, it may force them into circulation, acting, not merely as the embodiment of a general agreement, but as a legal compulsion—just as the law may enforce any enactment in regard to the ransfer of property. It may even force those who have already made contracts to take them instead of the dollars they bargained for. But there is no way in which it can, in subsequent bargains, regulate the purchasing power of a coin any more than that of a bushel of wheat. The law might call a bushel of wheat legal tender for five dollars, but, except under existing contracts, a bushel of wheat would buy no more boots or blankets than before. The seller would simply regulate his prices so as to get as much wheat for his goods as he thought them worth. If he thought his boots were worth four bushels of wheat, he would put the price at $20. If wheat became so valuable that three bushels were worth the boots, his price would be $15. And so, while the *prices* of all commodities would be adjusted with reference to the legal tender value of a bushel of wheat, the real *purchasing power* of the latter would not be increased. The only effect of the law would be that every seller must take wheat as dollars—the amount of it he would take for his goods remaining an open question between himself and his customer. It is just so with paper currency. It can be made current by law but not valuable. Its purchasing power will depend on the takers estimate of what it is worth at the time, or what it is likely to be worth in the near future. But over and above all this theory, which we think is sound and incontrovertible in itself, we have the undoubted historical *fact* that no law of legal tender has ever been able to make and keep "greenback" currencies as good as gold, when circumstances have tended to depreciate their value.

The only method that would seem likely to give value to these notes would be to force people to sell their property when asked, and to fix the price by law. Now the French are a logical people and they tried this plan once. In 1793 a law was passed fixing maximum prices in their depreciated paper currency for commodities and making sales compulsory. It was of course a measure of confiscation—but did it work?

The purchasing value of *assignats* continued to go down, in spite even of this law. Another was added, forbidding the purchase of gold for paper. Still *assignats* went down. In 1796 a franc in gold was worth 288 francs in paper. The price of a pound of candles in paper was 500 francs, and a ride in a hackney coach cost 600 ! A man who had borrowed 10,000 francs in gold in 1790 could now pay it back with 35 francs in gold ! Such was the result of the boldest and best contrived attempt ever made to evade the unbending laws of material and human nature.

It probably seemed to the legislators of the day that *their* laws, too, could not be evaded, but human nature proved too strong for them. Those who wished to change their depreciating paper for something that would retain its value, and so form a provision for the future, *would* have gold in spite of all laws. Those who feared legal robbery, in the form of maximum prices, refrained from taking their goods to market. Provisions grew scarce in the towns. The law was eluded, as all other laws are that directly oppose the general interest, and property continued to be exchanged for paper *assignats* at the value they bore in popular estimation—not that assigned to them by law.

Now this is what we have already gathered in reference to an inconvertible currency. Its very nature tends to affect it with suspicion, and consequently to depreciate it. It drives convertible currency out of circulation. If it continues to be issued, it must sooner or later exceed the demand for paper currency. When that occurs, its depreciation is certain, and will continue to be aggravated more and more by each new issue. This is the result of natural laws, and no legislation of any kind can prevent it. Such are its general characteristics. Let us now examine it more in detail.

It is a peculiar fact that, although one of the usual pleas for the introduction of such a currency is the real or supposed lack of circulating medium, and although it is the subsequent excess of the new currency which is largely the cause of its depreciation, yet that very depreciation is certain to bring about in turn a scarcity, and a renewed call for large issues. The consequence of depreciation is high prices, and prices, of manufactured articles at least, are apt to be increased even beyond the proper proportion for the time being, on account of the fear of further depreciation. The consequence of high prices is the necessity for a larger number of dollars, pounds, or francs for the transaction of any business which requires currency. As soon, therefore, as prices have reached their due proportion to the depression of the currency, the relations of circulation to business will become what they were before the issue. As soon as prices pass that proportion, the circulation will be relatively scarcer than it was before, and the cry will go up for more currency. It may seem, at first sight, as if this resultant scarcity should restore the value which the preceding excess had taken away. But we know from history that it does not, and a little reflection will show us why. Suppose the circulation of a community to consist of one million gold dollars, and that this is less than the needs of business require. Cut each dollar into three pieces and call each piece a dollar, and you will have a representation of a paper currency which has depreciated to 33⅓ cents on the dollar. There are three times as many dollars in circulation as there were before. But at the same time, by necessary consequence, prices have so increased that it takes three dollars to do the work that one had been doing, and so the scarcity is as great as before. If prices go any higher, the scarcity will become greater. Will the purchasing power of the pieces called dollars increase in consequence? Certainly not. Prices will, if they have gone above the due proportion, return to it again. If not, they will remain stationary. But each piece will only continue to buy just one third of what the whole dollar would have bought. The remedy for a scarcity of greenbacks is a new issue. The corresponding remedy in this case would be to cut each piece in two. Then prices would be six times as high as before the process of cutting began—as soon as they had time to adjust themselves—dollars would be six times as numerous—and currency still scarce. Of course, during the interval between each new issue and the adjustment of prices, there will be a time when each dollar will actually buy more than it is worth. These are times of easy "money markets," brisk business and high speculation. They are glorious times for the acute buyer, and for the dishonest borrower. The former knows he is getting more than he gives—the latter that he can repay his debts with less value than he has received, as soon as the currency has had time to settle to its new rate.

Such are times of "inflation." They always succeed large issues of inconvertible currency, and are always followed by periods of depression. And, since experience is a good teacher, the adjustment of prices takes less time after each issue, and the inflation period grows consequently shorter and shorter. The business system of a community is like the human system in this, that it gets accustomed to any stimulant, and the more frequently the stimulant is used the less effect it produces—in this respect too, that the succeeding depression is more profound after each stimulation.

The fact is, that if a community has not as much money as its cash transactions require, the only way to permanently relieve the inconvenience is to buy and put in circulation as much more money, or paper convertible into money, as is needed. The essential quality of money, both as a standard and an instrument to transfer property, is value. The essential quality of carts is carrying power; that of yard sticks is length. If there are not enough carts and yard sticks in a country to convey and measure its commodities, you cannot meet the want by substituting twice as many carts that each carry half as much as the old ones, or twice as many yard sticks each a foot and a half long. You must have more carts and more yard sticks of the same size as the old ones. If you have not dollars enough, you must meet the want by procuring more dollars as valuable as those you have. If the new carts or the new dollars were added to the old you might effect something, but an issue of inconvertible currency is a substitution and not an addition, since it drives more valuable currencies out of circulation. Everybody will use the cheaper currency to pay his debts. Besides, "Greenbacks" will not do for foreign exchanges, and consequently the more valuable currency is exported.

We have here the apparent anomaly that the scarcity of a currency does not increase its purchasing power in the same proportion that superabundance lessens it. If there are twice as many carts in a country as are needed to do its carrying, and all are kept in use, each will only do half a cart's work, and will only be worth half as much as if there were just enough. If there are only half enough carts, each will only be able to do one cart's work at the best, and half the carrying must remain undone, or be done by other means. But each cart will not be worth twice at much as if there were enough. The price will go up somewhat, from the competition to possess such a convenience, but not up to a point which would make it cheaper to use some other conveyance. It is almost so with dollars. If the number of dollars in use be twice too many, each will only do the work of half a dollar, and will only be worth half a dollar. If it be only half enough, each will be worth somewhat more than a dollar, from the competition to possess so convenient a medium of exchange, and so do somewhat more than the work of a dollar. But the increase of value and consequent working power will not be in proportion to the deficiency of the supply. It will only approach the point at which it would be cheaper to do without dollars and use cheques and bills of exchange, or to resort to barter. That is, dollars will be worth a certain premium, just as bills of exchange are, on grounds of convenience ; but the chief effect of the scarcity would be to prevent the use of dollars in some transactions in which they would otherwise be used.

An increased scarcity of *the metal gold* will proportionately increase the cost, and therefore the price, of gold coins, irrespective of their number, as a scarcity of wood will increase the price of carts irrespective of their number. But an increased scarcity of *gold coins* will not increase their price in the ratio of their scarcity, if the metal of which they are made have not become scarcer and dearer in the same proportion. In one case the increased price will directly follow the actual cost—for cost and price are convertible terms in regard to money. In the other, it will depend on the desire of the public to use that particular instrument of exchange in preference to others, and on the cost of making new coins or substitutes therefor. In the case of inconvertible currency a scarcity could lead to hardly any increase in price, as the material for, and manufacture of, such currency are both so cheap.

We see, then, that not only do successive issues of inconvertible paper tend to depreciate, but that each creates the demand for further inflation, without permanently filling any deficiency that may have originally existed in the circulating medium. It is like trying to fill a cistern above the

escape pipe. You may do so for a time, but the water will
soon come back to the old level. Morever, even if all other
currency were excluded, and inconvertible paper issued to
an extent less than the actual needs of the country, its increased value from the scarcity would not make up for the
lack of volume.

Although the general tendency of such a currency is towards depreciation, it has its ups and downs like other
variable commodities. Any political event that shakes or
strengthens public confidence in the government has a
corresponding effect on its value. A battle lost, a large foreign
debt incurred, a hint of repudiation, on the one hand—a
victory or a rumor of resumption on the other, may send the
price of " greenbacks " up or down to a frightful extent in
one day. While such events are rife, the taker of " greenbacks " is a gambler. By the estimate he puts on their value
he is practically betting on the chances of a rise or fall. This
may be very good amusement for the professional gamblers,
the dealers in gold, stock brokers, and all who are in the
habit of betting on variable values. But to the ordinary
trader, investor, or farmer, it is simply ruinous. He is forced
to gamble whether he will or not. He can never take a
dollar bill without incurring the risk of loosing an indefinite
number of cents. He must exchange his goods or produce
for an unknown quantity. It is as unsatisfactory as if " a
pound " or " a bushel " or " an acre " had no fixed meaning. In that case, the man who bought a ton of iron to-day,
might find it to-morrow so shrunk in weight that he could
bring it home in a wheelbarrow. The miller who contracted
for fifty bushels of wheat, might have it delivered next week
in two or three bags. The land speculator might find
that his fifty acres were only enough for a calf pasture.
What community could carry on business under these
conditions ? How long would the public endure the
authorization of a peculiar yard stick that grew shorter
every time a new batch were stamped and put in
use ? Or of an india rubber one that could be stretched
or contracted by every sharp manipulator ? Or how would
they like the declaration that the height of the mercury in a
barometer was a yard—no matter how atmospheric conditions might elevate or reduce it ? How many would use

a contractible cart that would carry a ton one day and only a hundred weight the next? How many buyers would approve of weights that would lose by evaporation every day in summer? Yet the law of legal tender is the "weights and measures act" of money, and a variable currency is as absurd and intolerable as a barometric yard stick, a contractible cart, or a volatile pound weight. The man who contracts for dollars when they are worth a certain percentage, and receives dollars worth a less percentage, is cheated by the operation of the law just as truly as he who contracts for any merchantable commodity and gets short weight or measure. Nay more, since dollars are the means of buying other commodities, the value of everying that is for sale is affected just as much by a variable currency as if all weights and measures were uncertain. An unit of measure, to be a rational contrivance, must be equal in extension to the unit of length of the thing weighed or measured—above all, it must remain of the same weight or size all the time. And this is just as mathematically true of the measuring tool called money as of other tools of the same description. One yard-stick will measure any number of yards, and one dollar will measure any number of dollars' worth, one by one; but the length of the one and the value of the other must be equal to the length or value measured at each application.

Worst of all, perhaps, is the fact that this variable tool of exchange does not in its variations affect equally all who use it. A weatherwise man may foretell the fluctuations of the barometer, and so may a speculator or a merchant foretell the fluctuations of "greenbacks." He understands the atmospheric laws of trade and currency. But most of those who use "greenbacks" know as little of why they go up or down, or when they are likely to do so, as a child does of the causes and times of the ebb and flow of the mercury. The average farmer, laborer, and small trader is completely at the mercy of the expert operator in all transactions in "greenbacks," and it is these classes who loose most by a variable currency. The same classes would loose, for the same reasons, by the barometrical or elastic yard-stick. The farmer, however well posted, has a special disadvantage, in the fact that he does not get his returns as quickly as a manufacturer or other trader. He must invest seed, labor and wages, in spring or in the previous autumn, and take the chances of what his grain may be worth in October. When currency is going down, he thus pays out dollars more valuable than those he will get in return. Besides, the price of his grain *in paper* is largely ruled by its price *in gold* in the world's markets, to which it ultimately finds its way. It follows from all this, that the prices of labor and farm produce are not likely to advance in the same proportion as the prices of things that are bought by the farmer and labourer. And this we find is borne out by universal experience. In France, for example, during the currency of *assignats*, while speculators were rolling in unaccustomed wealth and luxury, it was found necessary in the towns to spend large sums from the municipal funds to save the laborers from starvation. In the United States, the official returns from New England shew that, while the cost of living had doubled under a greenback currency, the price of land had remained stationary, and that of labor had but slightly increased. It appears then that the appropriate motto for an inconvertible note would be—"To him that hath shall be given more abundantly ; but from him that hath not shall be taken away even that which he hath."

It has been noted that the high prices of inflation times create a demand for new issues, in spite of the swollen state of the currency, and so further depress the value of the latter. The same cause forces these new issues at a disadvantage to the Government. As soon as it is known that a new issue is coming out, the barometer of price shows, by its rise, the effect of the coming change. When the deluge is actually flowing, its movement becomes rapid. Consequently the Government gets for its obligations, not only less than could be got for gold, but less after each issue than before. It is like the case of a man drifting towards bankruptcy. He effects loan after loan, but the very fact of his borrowing so much diminishes his credit, even where his actual circumstances are not known. The proceeds of each loan are less and less than the last, he has to borrow again to pay the interest—and at last the day comes when all these obligations must be met in cash as far as his assets will go. This means certain ruin for himself, and more or less of loss to his creditors. When his assets are all spent, he is allowed by law to "repudiate" the balance of his debt and start afresh. Such is the course that a nation must run when once fairly started on the current of inflation. There is the difference, apparently in its favor, that it can force credit, that is, it can compel its citizens to lend it value for its obligations, which the trader cannot do. But this only makes its course towards complete involvement more certain. The trader must stop borrowing when his credit is exhausted, and this may happen even before his assets are all covered by his obligations. The nation can go on borrowing by the issue of greenbacks as long as it sees fit—or until it be stopped by a revolution. But though it can continue to force its paper, it gets less and less for it each time, while the obligations themselves remain binding to their full face value. Thus, at one time in the United States, the issue of $1,000 in greenbacks would only buy for the government $333⅓ dollars worth of supplies, while the obligation remained to pay the whole $1,000. The case was infinitely worse in France in 1796 when *assignats* stood compared with gold as 1 to 288.

Now of course there is a limit in practice to this reckless borrowing, though there is none in theory. At some time financiers will get frightened at the worthlessness to which they have reduced the currency, and will decide to stop further issues. They must also at some period decide whether they will attempt to pay what they owe their citizens, or repudiate in whole or in part If they pay, we have seen that they must pay as much more than they received for each instalment as the currency had depreciated at the time of its issue. The United States have now to pay $100 for every $33⅓ in value received, for those issues of greenbacks that were floated at the worst period of the war. And who pays this? The people of course. The very individuals who have already suffered from the variations and degradation of greenbacks have now to meet at their face value obligations which procured so little. That is, there is a final dead loss to the country—besides the temporary losses to individuals—of two dollars in solid value out of every three of that issue. Could a nation possibly effect a loan on worse terms than the repayment of three dollars for one received?

It was this prospect that gave great strength to the agita-

tion against resumption—and no wonder that it did. But
fate is inexorable. There was no choice except to pay or repudiate. And what does repudiation mean to the people?
Simply the loss of whatever value they have given for the
greenbacks they hold.

It seems, then, that as the nation itself is the debtor
to those of its citizens who hold greenbacks, there is no
relief to the nation in a wiping out of its currency debt,
as there is to the individual bankrupt who has " gone through
the Court." The people as a whole would lose more by this
course than by honest payment—they would lose the *whole*
nominal value of their currency instead of the greater part of
it only. When a currency has once become depreciated there
is, therefore, no honest or dishonest course open to the nation
less costly than to redeem, at their face value, obligations for
which only a percentage of that value has been received.

We have so far dealt chiefly with the direct injuries of a
currency which is variable and intrinsically of little value.
Are there any which arise from the conditions of trade
and society which such a currency generates? Reason,
and the facts that have been under our own eyes for
years, answer " yes, and great ones." In the intervals
between new issues of paper and the consequent adjust-
ments of prices, speculation is naturally rife. Such
times are the paradise of the promoter of companies,
the inexperienced but ambitious trader, the Col. Sellars
who sees " millions " in every new enterprise. Each flow
of the tide floats such drift wood a little higher up the
beach, each ebb leaves them stranded a little further above
high water-mark. We all remember how vastly active were
all enterprises and industries in the United States for some
time after the war. There was no end of capital—or rather
of doubtful currency pretending to represent capital—for investment in anything. Railways were begun, with one end
in civilization and the other stretching out vaguely towards
" Sundown." All manufacturing establishments were taxed
to the utmost to furnish material for new undertakings.
Labor was in fair demand. Everything bore the appearance
of the busiest prosperity. But it was the prosperity of the
spendthrift, who makes business lively around him as long
as the paternal acres last. The nation was living on its

credit, and even drawing bills on posterity. And then—just when such a large proportion of all it could borrow, as well as all it had saved, was invested in works that yielded no immediate revenue—the crash came. Universal depression, and the necessity for resumption, overtook the country at the same time. It was as if a reckless speculator had been called on to pay his debts, just at the moment when his whole resources were involved in complicated and risky operations. The railroads might prove profitable at some time, but they afforded no present means of realizing hard cash. The investments in land and machinery, which had been made in the heat and whirlwind of inflation, shrunk in price. The fictitious value with which speculation had endowed commodities in general vanished. In short, the spendthrift found himself at the end of his tether, and reduced from careless luxury to the necessity of quiet, living and the careful saving of what little remained to him. The shock to business in general was terrific, and the prostration has lasted longer there than in any other country which has felt the "hard times" But that which was only a loss of wealth and luxury to some was ruin to others. The laboring classes and the farmers were left almost helpless. They had never shared in the inflation of values to the same extent as the others. The price of what they bought had always gone up faster than that of their labor or produce. The price of the farmer's grain was ruled by its price in Liverpool. The New-York dealer gave no more for what he bought to export than for what he bought to sell at home. Grain sold, in paper, at little above the gold price, while all farmers' supplies cost fancy figures in greenbacks. And yet these classes suffered at least as much in percentage as the speculator by the bursting of the bubble—more in actual proportion, for it was sometimes their all. Land fell in price, not only from the fall of greenbacks, but from the slackening of operations that had caused a demand for it. Produce fell like other things. Labor not only fell off in price, but became a drug in the market. The inordinate speculations of past years had drawn thousands to the country who had now absolutely nothing to do. Hence we find the startling phenomenon, in a young and half-peopled country, of violent and universal strikes amongst poverty stricken laborers. Hence we see that the stream of emigration to a country possessing vast stretches of unoccupied land nearly ran dry—nay more, that streams began to trickle back to the over-peopled countries of Europe.

That country is now recovering, as any country with such resources must recover sooner or later. But it has paid an enormous price, directly in hard cash, and indirectly in commercial and industrial losses, for its brief fool's paradise of living on credit.

And it is not certain that the social demoralization caused thereby will bear no evil fruits in the future. The people have tasted the intoxication of the spendthrift's life. They have had to forego it for a time. But many still long for the violent excitements of speculation,—the chances that a lottery of values opens to the clever and unprincipled—and we may expect some effort to bring about a similar condition of things again. The moral sense of the nation has been blunted by the use of dishonest weights and measures for all commodities, and we may have to wait for a new generation to see it restored.

We must observe that there are conditions under which a certain issue of inconvertible notes may be almost, or quite, harmless. They are such conditions as shall make those notes in public estimation nearly or quite equal to convertible ones, or at least constant in value even if somewhat depreciated. It is the variation that does the principal mischief. Such conditions are of course quite exceptional. A very strong government, in temporary difficulties, may sometimes issue, to a very patriotic people, a comparatively small quantity of such paper without much injury. In these circumstances the people will put the credit of the issuer very high, and take but little account of the postponement of a debt considered so thoroughly good. Such exceptional conditions occurred in England early in this century. In consequence of the French war debt, Bank of England notes were made for a time inconvertible, which practically amounted to an issue of greenbacks. Everybody trusted the Bank's credit, but for a time there was an excess of circulation and a consequent depreciation. A guinea of 21 shillings was worth at one time 27 shillings in paper. But he fates were again propitious to the Bank. Two hundred and fifty private banks failed, and their issues went out of use—so contracting the currency. The circumstances of the country began to demand more circulation, and finally the bank was able to resume payment in gold. without loss, in 1821, two years earlier than required by law. It will be seen that the salvation of this currency lay in the high credit of the issuer, in the caution with which it was issued, and in the accidental increase in demand which helped to employ it.

The extent to which the price of greenbacks in the United States was at the mercy of speculators, at certain periods, was frightful. In a country that has foreign dealings a certain quantity of gold is always needed for exchange purposes. Greenbacks, by driving gold out of circulation, caused it to be exported, and there was always the necessity for a certain effort to secure the amount required. With a convertible currency there is no such temptation to export gold, and no such scarcity for the uses of commerce. As New York is the chief centre of the export and import trade, it was there that the struggle usually took place for the supply of gold on the market, and there consequently that the price of gold for the day was fixed, which, in turn, fixed the price of greenbacks.

It appears, then, that the price of the latter was subject to depreciation not only from excess, or lack of confidence, but also from a temporary scarcity of gold for commercial use. This was a grand opening for the "Bulls" and "Bears" of Wall street, and they took full advantage of it. When it was foreseen that shipments of gold must shortly be made, it was the easiest thing in the world to "corner" the visible supply—that is, to buy up the greater part of it. Then, when settlement day came, the importer or banker must pay a premium for it, proportioned to the artificial scarcity. He could not wait till a fresh supply arrived, short as the time might be. He must remit on a certain day to save his credit. Consequently, if the generality of dealers had failed to make provision in time, there would be a sudden and sometimes enormous rise in gold. The telegraph hourly carried the news to all parts of the country, and every transaction involving the exchange of greenbacks for value was affected thereby. The increase might be, and usually was, only temporary, and the gain or loss to the brokers and

3

merchants of New York might make very little difference to the country at large. But it must be remembered that every fluctuation in greenbacks meant an actual increase or decrease in the cash value of all commodities, until prices could be re-adjusted. The shorter the term of the fluctuation, the less chance there was of such re-adjustment. If gold went up 25 per cent. on Friday, it was almost impossible for every merchant and farmer to put up his prices 25 per cent. on Saturday, and yet, unless he did so, he was selling at a loss. Of course, if he did not use the proceeds of his sales at once, gold might come down again and paper go up, but in the complicated and rapid transactions of modern commerce, immediate realization, and instant use of cash are often necessary. It follows then that not only the price of greenbacks, but the actual cash value of all commodities, were temporarily at the mercy of the gold room speculators. Their power for evil was just as real as if they had been able to reduce for the day a man's stock of goods—the extent of his farm—the bushels in his granary.

As we have said, fluctuations from this cause must usually be temporary. Gold is very portable, and a general scarcity of it almost impossible. Any deficiency is, therefore, soon filled, but in the meantime an incalculable amount of mischief may be done. It is clear that no such evils could result from a temporary and local scarcity of gold under a convertible currency. Those who had to buy at once might have to pay a high premium, but that would be the extent of the loss. The convertible currency could not be injured; if anything, it would rise, though we find by experience that it is not usually affected at all.

Besides this cornering of gold required for immediate use, there was a wide field for gambling in buying gold for a slower rise in price, and this too tended to demoralize business. In this case the buyers' hopes rested on such chances as might lessen the value of the currency—defeats, new issues and the like—and it was the paper, not the gold on whose fluctuations he was really betting.

CHAPTER III.

PAPER CURRENCY IN FRANCE.*

The nature and evils of a currency not convertible at will into specie may best be realized by a connected study of its history in some one community. The author has chosen the history of the *assignats* in France for a study of this kind, for several reasons. The experiment was begun there under fairly favorable circumstances—not as a last resort against national bankruptcy. It was carried out by men of exceptional ability, and what is more, it was carried out to all its logical conclusions. That history seems a perfect study of what can be done with the best contrived inconvertible currency, backed by all the legal appliances that ingenuity can suggest, and by the most arbitrary exercise of power. It is well worth while then to take a connected view of it, even at the risk of some slight repetition.

Near the end of 1789 France was embarassed, deeply but by no means hopelessly. Late events had made capital timid, and there was a general feeling of uneasiness which led to business stagnation. Economy, and a waiting policy, might have cured all this, but such a policy was not congenial to the spirit of the times. The idea that more circulation was wanted came to the front then, as naturally as in all times of depression. The cry for paper currency went up, as it has so often gone up nearer home, in the hope that there might be more money to lend, and a general revival of prosperity. Necker, and other thoughtful men in the Assembly, opposed this cry, but it was based on popular prejudice, and proved too strong for argument. On April 19th 1790, the Finance Committee reported in favor of the desired issues. Its arguments are worth remembering. It said that " the people demand a new circulating medium "; that " the circulation

---

*The historical part of the following account is condensed from a pamphlet written by Andrew D. White, L. L. D., President of Cornell University, and based on the original authorities.

of paper money is the best of operations"; that "it is the most free, because it reposes on the will of the people"; and that "it will bind the interests of the citizens to the public good." It went on ; "Let us show to Europe that we understand our own resources ; let us immediately take the broad road to our liberation, instead of dragging ourselves along the tortuous and obscure path of fragmentary loans." It recommended, in conclusion, a carefully guarded issue of 400,000,000 francs. It was urged in support of this that "paper money under a despotism is dangerous, but under a constitutional government, which duly regulates its use, this danger disappears." A political argument was stronger still. The nation had just confiscated the real estate of the French Church, comprising estates, churches, palaces, conventual buildings, and other property in town and country, to the value of about 4,000,000,000 francs, or more than one third of the real estate of France. It was proposed to make these lands the security for the new issue. This it was thought would attain two ends. It would be an easy way of relieving pressing wants, and the conversion of the notes into land would create a large class of small holders, committed to the government which gave them their title. The currency would increase business and foster sales of public lands—the proceeds of the sales would furnish new funds—all was bright and hopeful for the patriot and the financier.

The currency was issued in April, 1790 in the form of *assignats,* mortgages on the nation's real estate, bearing interest at three per cent. Nothing could seem sounder. A mortgage on good real estate is the best of securities, and a mortgage-currency which bore interest was surely the most attractive kind of inconvertible paper. No wonder some asserted that it would prove more valuable than gold, and that others called it *papier-terre*—"paper real estate." The notes bore on their face fine engravings, and calculations of the amount of interest accruing daily to the holder. The Assembly issued an address to the people, setting forth the advantages of the new currency. "The nation was delivered by this grand means from all uncertainty, and from all ruinous results of the credit system—incessantly a prey to the caprices of cupidity." "Paper money is without inherent value, unless it represents some special property. Without representing some special property it is inadmissable in trade to compete

with a metallic currency, which has a value. real and independent of the public action ; *therefore it is that the paper
money which has only the public authority as its basis has
always caused ruin where it has been established ;* that is the
reason why the bank notes of 1720, issued by John Law, after
having caused terrible evils, have only left frightful
memories. Therefore it is that the National Assembly has
not wished to expose you to this danger, but has given this
new paper money, not only a value derived from the national
authority, but a value *real, immutable,* a value which permits
it to sustain advantageously a comparison with the precious
metals themselves." × × " These *assignats* bearing interest as they do will soon be considered better than the coin
now hoarded, and will again bring it out into circulation."
Such a currency, issued by statesmen who showed such a
correct knowledge of a part of the question, must have seemed
the best substitute possible for one redeemable in coin.

For a time its effects were all that could be desired. The
government was relieved, and business of all kinds felt the
increased circulation, in the manner we have already noticed
when treating of inconvertible issues in general. Objectors
were silenced and the " *assignat* men " were triumphant.
Perhaps, had the issue stopped here, the result might have
been no worse than we have seen it was in England. But
just here came in the law already pointed out, that one issue
inevitably calls for another. In four months the government
was again short of means, and the country was again short
of currency. The debate in the Assembly was renewed, and
another report was drafted. It concluded that the issue
already made had proved successful, and that, though there
might be some danger in the way, it was necessary above all
to "save the country." Mirabeau insisted that if the paper
became too abundant it would be absorbed in buying
national lands, and compared the process to the cycle of
evaporation and rainfall. Abbé Gouttes declared that paper
money "would supply a circulating medium which will
preserve public morals from corruption !" A writer in the
press argued thus : "The earth is the source of all value.
You cannot distribute the earth in a circulating value, but
this paper becomes representative of that value, and it is
evident that the creditors of the nation will not be injured by
taking it." Mirabeau finished the struggle. He declared that

the notes were better secured than if redeemable in specie; that the precious metals were only employed in the secondary arts, while the new money represented the most real of all property, the source of all production, the *land* itself. No other nation that had tried paper money had been so fortunate as to be able to give a mortgage security for it. Whoever took French money had a mortgage on saleable property, instead of a vague claim upon the nation. "He cried "I would rather have a mortgage on a garden than on a kingdom." Another issue of 800,000,000 francs was made, with the stipulation that the whole amount in circulation was never to exceed 1,200,000,000 francs, and that all notes returned to the Treasury should be burned. This was a full committal to the policy of inflation, and the regular results soon, followed. Ere long the people cried again for more currency, and the safe-guards just mentioned were broken through. 160,000,000 francs, returned to the Treasury, were re-issued as small notes. This only whetted the public appetite. The craving for stimulants was growing fiercer, and, in less than nine months after the giving of solemn pledges against undue expansion, another issue of 600,000,000 francs was floated. This was in June 1791. The first and second issues had passed with great difficulty. Now the delusion had gained momentum, and this third bill passed with little objection.

Immediately a depreciation of eight or ten per cent. took place. Of course every cause but the real one was adduced by the inflationists. The country people must be ignorant of the beauties of paper currency. An address was voted to enlighten them. Then gold began to disappear, as we have seen it always does retreat before an inferior currency. The popular voice cried "coin will keep rising till the people hang a broker." Others would have it that the Bourbons were sending specie away through some mysterious channel to the centres of their intrigues abroad. Others were sure that English emissaries were sapping public confidence in the currency, and more than one suspected person suffered. Talleyrand said it was because the exports were too small and the imports too large. He took the actual phenomenon for the cause of itself, for this excess of imports was caused by the fact that it paid to export gold, or, in other words, to buy abroad with coin instead of produce.

Gold was hoarded too of course. Those who hoarded it were branded as criminals worthy of death. It was held to be the duty of every honest citizen to give his gold for paper.

Manufactures began to suffer. They had been stimulated of course by the first issues, but now they felt the effects of high prices and unfavorable exchanges. One after another stopped. High protective duties were tried. All was in vain. Workmen were idle by thousands, and general distress prevailed. The expulsion of so many clever artizans by the edict of Nantes, and the shiftlessness of Louis XV., had failed to seriously injure French industry. This tampering with the currency wrought more evil to it in a few months than all other causes in a century. Values had become totally unsettled. No one could tell what a 100 fr. bill might be worth in a month. Capitalists declined to invest. Enterprise was checked. The demand for labor was still further diminished. Of course the poor became more straitened proportionately than the rich. Every purchase of supplies became a speculation. Even Louis Blanc, the apologist of revolutionary statesmanship. admits that " commerce was dead—betting took its place."

A worse symptom still was the obliteration of that thrift so intensely characteristic of the French people. With plenty of currency which was not certain to "keep" the motives of economy disappeared, and luxury became the rule. Stock gambling spread from the great centres to the smallest hamlets. Many small fortunes, hardly earned by agriculture or mechanical industry, were melted down into huge fortunes for the dropsical plutocracy of the *bourse.* Society was demoralized. Politicians hitherto held immaculate began to take bribes.

Another threatening outgrowth now appeared. This was the vast debtor class, who had a direct interest in depreciating the currency in which their debts were to be paid. Those who had bought government lands and made small payments formed the nucleus of it. All who had gone deeply in debt during the inflation joined them. They ruled the clubs—wrote in the press—got into the assembly—and soon the debtors pervaded all ranks, clamoring for more currency, and debauching the common sense of the people. They nursed the superstition that is always born in such circumstances—that which leads the ignorant to believe that all will come right if only *enough* paper is issued. The drunkard, when his usual draught fails to exhilarate, says "if I only take *enough* it will put me all right again." The poor. who suffer from the "blues" that succeed inflation, say "if we only had *enough* currency we should all be rich."

All hopes of checking the current now vanished. In December 1791 a new issue of 300,000,000 francs came from the printing press.

Then came to light the new system of political economy which patriotic Frenchmen had to invent to suit their actual circumstances. It was held, about this time, that a depreciated currency, which would only circulate at home, was a blessing. It separated France from other nations, and saved her from the evils of too wide a commerce, which was a curse to any country. It kept money at home, and encouraged home manufactures. "Old fashioned ideas should not fetter the free French citizen of the eighteenth century." Truly there are no new delusions under the sun!

A fifth issue came out in April 1792, to the extent of another 300,000,000. About the same time, Cambon sneered at public creditors, who might be supposed to be injured thereby, as " rich people, old financiers, and bankers." Payment of dues to all public creditors for large amounts was suspended. This was of course intended to save money for the poor. But unfortunately the poor suffered more than ever. No one who had capital would risk it in productive employment, but tried to put it in some permanent form where it would retain its value. Labor was a drug. Wages, in the summer of 1792, remained where they had been four years before—at 15 sous a day—while all other prices had gone up enormously. In December 1792 there were 2,800,-000,000 francs in paper in circulation.

Then came the confiscation of the estates of the *Emigrés*, reckoned at three billion francs. New issues were based upon these on the old plea. In 1793 things approached a crisis. Demagogues declaimed against the corruption of ministers, the intrigues of the emigrant nobles, the monopolizing spirits of the merchants, against everything but the real cause of the distress. A tax was laid on the rich by the National Convention, to the extent of 400,000,000 francs, to buy bread for the poor. Marat declared that if a few shop-keepers were hanged and their shops, plundered the people would be relieved. The people took his advice, and the plundering mob had to be bought off by a grant of 7,000,000 francs. And then the Jacobin Club called for a law to equalize the values of paper and coin.

It was at this crisis that the governing body decided to go to all lengths to float the currency. They had already made pieces of paper *francs* by law. They would now also define how much each seller must give for a franc. They passed laws fixing maximum prices for all commodities, and imposing penalties on those who refused to sell at such prices. This is the most courageous and logical act on record, on the part of inflationists. Of course it was confiscation and monstrous tyranny, but what of that? Was it not necessary to complete the work they had begun—that of making a currency valuable, to which the public did not attach value for its own sake? A country which issues an inconvertible currency and makes it legal tender, has taken the first step which logically involves a law of maximum prices. What is the use of making paper francs, if you can't make each buy a franc's worth? And is it greater tyranny to say to a seller "you *must* take so many paper francs for your goods," than to say to a lender "you *must* take 100 paper francs now, worth but ten in gold, for the hundred that were borrowed from you when they were worth their face in gold?" Any inconvertible currency works confiscation from time to time on individuals. It was logical, and no worse than the rest of the system, to try to equalize the confiscation all round.

But another avenue of escape had yet to be stopped. People bought gold with *assignats*, and hoarded it as the the only safe investment. This was forbidden under penalty of six years imprisonment.

In spite of all these extreme measures *assignats* continued to fall. Why? They were well secured on choice real estate, worth about five per cent. of revenue in ordinary times, to which the people believed their government could give a good title. Why then did not their convertibility into land save them? John Stuart Mill points out that their conversion into land would be an investment in land, and this was beyond the means of most of those who handled the currency. It passed into the hands of the largest classes as wages, or the price of produce. It passed out again for

the necessaries of life. What sort of investment in land
could the laborer make with his 15 sous per day ? What
amount of land could even the well to do farmer buy with
his year's profits? And what did most of those who handled
the currency *want* with land ? It is clear that only such
notes as represented spare funds could be invested at all, and
that only considerable amounts of such capital could be invested to advantage. Besides, the amount required for circulation must stay in circulation, and could not be converted into
anything but coin, which would take its place in exchanges.
Now we have seen that the most enormously increased circulating medium is sooner or later absorbed by the high
prices it generates, and serves the public wants no better
than a smaller quantity. It follows that no increase of
currency could leave a surplus for conversion into land,
beyond the natural amount of spare capital, except during
the time between its issue and the adjustment of prices.

Convertibility into land having failed, convertibility into
interest bearing bonds was tried. This failed too for exactly
the same reason. More savage compulsory laws were en-
acted. Still *assignats* went down. The national debt was
virtually repudiated. Still they kept on their downward
course. Good harvests did them and the country no service.
After the unusually fine crop of 1794 came a winter of famine
in the towns. Farmers would not come to market to be
robbed by the " maximum " laws. At the end of July, 1795,
we find 16,000,000,000 francs of paper in circulation—100 of
which were worth 2½ of gold—and still a " lack of currency "—the chronic craving of the currency-drunkard. Then
came an apparent revival of business. Holders of assignats
were seized with a rage of self-preservation—they *must* buy
something with them that would not depreciate. Real estate,
gold, and everything durable were briskly demanded by
those who had any savings to secure. In February, 1796,
36,000,000,000 of assignats were in circulation, and 1 franc in
gold was worth 288 in paper. Sugar was worth 500 francs a
pound, soap 230 fr., candles 140 fr. A ride in a hackney
coach cost 600 francs.

Where were the maximum laws all this time, with their
value giving powers? They were perhaps keeping company
with Mrs. Partington and her mop—exchanging condolences
on their common inability to defy the forces of nature. They

may have, here and there, "come down" on some poor
fellow who risked his liberty to get his living, but they were
utterly powerless to coerce the nation into parting with its
property for less than it was worth.

Then the issue of *assignats* was stopped and *mandats* took
their place. *Mandats* were convertible, without any form of
foreclosure or purchase, into choice government lands, up to
their face value. It was held that these were a vast improvement on the clumsy invention that preceded them.
They were as much better as deeds are better than mortgages. Instantly after their issue they began, however, to
follow the *assignats* on the down grade. Laws were passed
imposing a fine of one thousand livres on who ever decried
them. People ceased decrying *mandats*, but increased the
discount on them.

This was the last dying struggle of inflation. When
mandats failed, all hope was lost, and it was acknowledged
that the country must pay or repudiate. To pay thirty-six,
billion *assignats* and twenty-five million *mandats* was impossible. On July 16th, 1796, it was decreed that all paper
should pass at its real value, and that bargains might be
made in any currency. The whole issue was repudiated.

We have given some considerable time and space to this
historical study, but it has perhaps been worth our while.
It has illustrated many of our previous arguments, and may
furnish material for future ones. At all events, it has been
instructive to note the utter failure of a long continued, des-
perate, logical, and systematic effort to get clear of the
intangible clinging fetters of economic laws. The men who
struggled against these laws were fanatical enthusiasts
perhaps, but they were *thorough* for that very reason. No
scruples, no traditions, held them back from any expedient
that might seem likely to affect their ends. And what is
more, they were *successful* enthusiasts in most things they
undertook. The people of France in those days were
victorious over every opponent but natural law, and if they
failed to conquer this, it was because law was strong—not
because France was weak. The currency of *assignats* and
mandats was in its nature the strongest to all appearance
that could be constructed short of a gold basis. As a
security it was strong in fact as well as appearance. But
we have seen how it lacked the essential of a currency. *It was*

convertible only into something which could not itself be used as currency. Such paper is perhaps worse than the unsecured obligations of a government. Nothing could be got for it from the issuer but what it professed to secure to the holder. If he did not want land or bonds the government would give him nothing. It was as liable to depreciation as unsecured issues to the same amount. It was not as likely as unsecured paper to recuperate with returning national prosperity. It fell in spite of its perfect security for payment in land or bonds. No circumstances, which still left it convertible into those things only, could renew its value.

CHAPTER IV.

SUPPLY OF CURRENCY.

We have asked already, and answered in a general way, the question "How much *money* does a community need?" We may now ask "How much currency of all kinds, including paper, is enough?" We have been considering cases where the supply was evidently too great—how can a government avoid issuing an over supply? What rule can it go by? The answer is the same as to the question about money. As much currency as the people of any country will buy in the open market, without any legal pressure being laid upon them, is enough for that country. To force more than this upon them is to decrease and render variable the value of the currency, and so make it totally unfit to be used as a currency at all. If the market be left free and open, and provision be made for supplying as much currency as the people will buy, the community will keep itself always supplied with what currency it needs, without any care or management whatever on the part of the government. If the furnishing of any part of the currency be left to private enterprise—as is the case with bank notes—it is certain that, in regard to that part at least, the public will be thoroughly supplied with all they call for, and that no government interference is needed.

In short, the currency maker, if he wish to supply his market fully without glutting it, must follow the same course as the maker of axes or any other tool or commodity. No one can say beforehand how many axes will fill the market, but the forge and anvil are kept busy so long as axes continue to sell freely, and the axe-maker studies to keep rather behind than in advance of the demand. It is better for him to have to make a few hundred extra, after he thought all orders had ceased, than to have the same number left on his hands. Coin and notes of all kinds are sold just as literally as axes, since they are always issued in exchange for value. The maker and vendor of currency must, therefore, study the market just as any other manufacturer does, knowing that the consequences of an over supply will be equally disastrous to his business.

We have seen that anything like a permanent excess, or glut, of gold and convertible notes is impossible. The excess, of gold immediately flows out of the country in exchange for other commodities. The excess of convertible notes is immediately turned into gold and—if there were gold enough without it—passes away as if it had been a direct issue of coin. It is only in the case of inconvertible notes that a permanent excess is possible, and we have seen that the circumstances attending the issue of these lead inevitably to excess. The sale of these notes is not a business transaction in any sense. It is a *forced* sale, without reference to demand, and it must be repeated whenever the seller—the government—wants funds, no matter how low the price may have fallen. The law of legal tender applied to such a currency has somewhat the effect of screwing down the safety valve of a boiler. The expansive volume of inconvertible notes cannot condense itself any more than so much hot steam, and, having no means of escape, must sooner or later burst something.

The question of the relative quantities of coin and paper, where both circulate together as currency, must also be settled by the popular demand for each. It has been held by some authorities that the right quantity for a mixed currency is one equal to the quantity of coin that would circulate if it were alone. How that quantity could be ascertained has never been disclosed. But, apart from this, there is no reason why a sound and useful circulation of paper, in excess, even largely in excess, of the probable circulation of coin alone, should not exist. Paper is vastly more convenient than coin for many purposes, and it is extremely likely that people will use more of it in daily transactions than they would of coin. As to the relative amounts of the two kinds of currency, it may be assumed that people will prefer the more convenient, for all purposes that it will serve. Gold will perhaps always be necessary to some extent for foreign remittances, but the paper, if it be thoroughly sound, is likely to be preferred for ordinary use. The relation of the volume of currency of all kinds to the amount of business done in a community is very variable. It depends altogether on the amount of work, that is circulation, done by each coin or note, and on the extent to which currency is superseded by other mediums of exchange. These conditions in turn vary with the nature and complexity of business transactions.

In densely peopled communities, where everyone deals with everyone else, currency circulates rapidly, and a comparatively small quantity is needed to square all transactions. A manufacturing town is a good example. The cash paid by the employers to their "hands" passes at once to the different tradesmen, and from these to other parties. Thus a single dollar may take part in fifty transactions in a week, and so do the work that would have required fifty different dollars if each only took part in one. In new settlements, on the other hand, where towns are few, and the commercial transactions of the people limited, currency is apt to stay long with each taker. Cash received for timber, or grain, or stock, is likely to be reserved for two or three occasions of laying in supplies, or for yearly payments on land and the like. Here of course a much larger volume of currency, in proportion to business, will be required than in cities. Certain trades and undertakings, again, require a larger supply of currency than others. They are those in which a large number of payments of comparatively small sums have to be made in cash. The produce trades, and public and other works employing unskilled labor outside of towns, may be cited as examples. Commercial transactions, on the contrary, require comparatively little. Large accounts between merchants and banks are squared to a great extent by means of cheques, drafts, bills of exchange, and similar substitutes for currency. Where all the conditions which diminish the demand for currency are present together the effect is astonishing. Perhaps this occurs nowhere else to such an extent as in the business part of London, England, commonly called " the City." The use of cheques is there highly developed. Not only do banks and business men use them in dealing with each other, but they are very common instruments of purchase at the shops, as the Londoner prefers keeping his cash in a bank and paying it out in this way. And this payment by cheque instead of with currency does not merely postpone the handling of the latter till the shopkeeper presents the cheques—it prevents it altogether in many cases. The shop-keepers have their own bank-accounts, pay in the cheques to their bankers, and receive credit therefor on the books. The bankers, instead of sending the cheques to be cashed at the banks on which they are drawn, send them to an institution called the " Clearing House." This is an office at which the accounts between the different banks are regulated. Every bank sends in cheques on some other bank, and here they are balanced against each other, and a list is drawn up several times a day of the cheques for and against each. At the close of the day each bank gives or receives a cheque on the Bank of England, for the balance against it or in its favor in its days dealings with every other bank. A banker may send in cheques for £100,000 and receive one for £50 only in settlement. This cheque finally goes to his credit in the Bank of England, and so a business of millions of pounds may be transacted without a single sovereign passing from hand to hand. Sir John Lubbock, the eminent banker, gives as an illustration of this an analysis of a sum of £19,000,000 paid in to his bank, as follows :

Cheques and bills...............£18,395,000
Notes.................................   487,000
Coin...................................   118,000

It is clear that "the City" requires very little currency compared with the volume of its business. The same is true to a less extent of England generally, and of large cities everywhere. If it were true that the amount of money and currency in circulation is a true test of the wealth of a community, the richest country in the world, and the very focus of its riches, would be rated wonderfully low as compared with the youngest of its colonies.

From all these considerations we may draw the conclusion that it is impossible to say in advance how much currency per head is enough for any community, or even what proportion it should bear to the volume of business. The only way to ascertain the right amount is to leave the currency market as free and open as the market for any other tool or commodity. All that a government can do is to secure the genuine goodness of the currency—whether the issue be made by itself or by others under its supervision.

CHAPTER V.

CURRENCY, CAPITAL AND INTEREST.

The currency question is seldom discussed, now-a-days, without the use of language which implies that there is some necessary relation between the quantity of currency in circulation and the amount and "price" of capital available for investment. This idea is in some cases the cause, and in others the consequence, of our familiarity with certain expressions which are not only incorrect but misleading. One of these is the use of the word "money," not only as a synonym for wealth generally, but as a name for all forms of capital available for investment, and for all accrued profits. To say that a man who owns large estates is "worth a lot of money" is a comparatively harmless figure of speech—just because every one sees that it *is* a figure of speech. But if the same phrase is used of a wealthy banker, or if one speaks of "cheap money" and "dear money"—of the "money market"—"scarcity of money in the country,"—the word "money" is almost sure to be taken in a literal sense, as meaning actual coin and notes. And yet in all these instances the use of that word in the latter sense is absolutely

incorrect, and conveys a totally false impression of the actual
state of things. When a man says money is cheap, he means
that loans can be had at low rates. When he speaks of the
money market, he means the market in which loans are
negotiated. When he speaks of a scarcity of money, he means
that it is hard to obtain loans or hard to collect debts, or that
people generally are poorer than usual. It is important then
to understand in what loans consist—what is borrowed from
banks and private parties—what is dealt in on the money
market—what it is that is really abundant when "money is
plenty," and scarce when "money is tight."

To say that it is "capital" is a poor explanation, unless we
define what capital is. Some authorities extend the meaning
of the word so as to include all the wealth-producing
capabilities of the individual—his labor, intelligence, and
energy, as well as his property. Others take it to mean that
part of a man's property which is not required for immediate
sustenance, and may be used for the production of other property—in short his *spare wealth.* However logical the wider
definition may be, it is in the latter sense that we generally
use the word. It is in this sense that we speak of capital
being invested, of capital being lent, of realized capital, since
it is only spare wealth which could be used in these ways.

Now it is *capital* in this sense, and *capital only,* that, is
borrowed, lent, invested, dealt in generally, on the so-called
money market—and not *money,* the instrument of exchange.
But it may be said "do not loans always take the form of
money?" Not always, as we shall see, but let us first consider
the cases where they do. A business man borrows one
thousand dollars. The money lender gives him that amount
in coin or notes for which he gets an obligation to repay
$1,000 with interest. The borrower of course has not borrowed
this money to lay it by in his safe. He intends to use it
in new purchases or in payment of debts—in either case to
exchange it for value received. If the transaction is a
legitimate business one, he intends to invest the cash in
some productive form. He may buy cotton machinery with
it, or silks and woollens to be retailed at a profit, or land, to
hold for a rise or to farm for his own benefit. But he cannot so invest the money without parting with it. As soon,
therefore, as he has put the money to its intended use it is
gone. When the transaction is complete we find that he

4

has in his possession, not the one thousand dollars he received from the lender, but one thousand dollars worth of goods
or "plant"—that amount in fact of capital in a productive
form. It is this capital then that he has borrowed, and not
the coins and notes that he actually received. It is just the
same thing, in effect, as if he had rented the goods or machinery from some one who had them. He would then have
to hand back the same, or an equal value in kind at the end of
his term, just as he now has to return an equal value in
money. During the term he would have full control of
what he rented for the purpose of making profit, just as he
has now full control of the capital to make profit of. In the
one case, as in the other, he would have to pay a certain sum
yearly for the use of what is lent him. One case is as real a loan
of capital as the other· When the loan passes in the form
of money, it is because the lender has not the articles which
the borrower requires, or does not find it convenient to lend
them. He therefore gives the borrower the means of purchasing whatever he wants, in the form of coin or notes.

Nothing can be more absurd than to reason as if it were
the actual currency that is borrowed in such transactions.
Why, a bank may, in an active business centre, handle the
same coins and notes ten times in a week—it may lend
them to borrowers, receive them in from other customers,
and lend them out again that number of times. And yet,
in each case it has made a loan for a considerable term
by means of those notes. Could it lend the same things
to ten different persons for three months each ? Certainly
not, but it can easily use the same instruments for conveying a certain value to each of ten persons within a week
— or within a day if circulation were rapid enough.

As soon as we understand that it is *capital* and not *currency* that is borrowed, we see what interest is, why it is
reasonable to charge interest, and what regulates the rate of
interest.

Interest is clearly the rent or hire of capital—a payment
of the same nature as wages of labor or the rent of land.
You pay a man wages because he gives you the benefit of
his labor. You pay a man rent because he gives you the
benefit of his land. You pay a man interest because he gives
you the benefit of his capital. It is reasonable to exact payment in all these cases. The laborer could work for himself,

·or other employers, if he were not working for you. He foregoes that source of profit and must be recouped. Besides, he gives you a direct value in his labor and must be paid for that. These are the two considerations that regulate wages in any particular case—what the laborer, could make ·or earn elsewhere, and what his labor is worth to the particular employer in question. The same considerations affect rent. The tenant here stands in the position of the employer. The owner foregoes certain profits that the land would yield to himself, and the tenant receives them instead. The rent, then, which is the payment in place of these profits, will ·depend on the productiveness of the land, other things being equal. Now a borrower hires or rents capital, which is wealth capable of being used productively. It is reasonable that he should pay the lender for the profits which the latter foregoes and he receives ; indeed he could get the use of capital on no other terms. The amount he will have to pay will depend, like the rent of land, on the productiveness of the property rented—that is on the average profits derivable from capital productively employed. The lender will require as much profit as he could make by using the capital himself, less a fair deduction for the trouble and risk which he avoids by lending. It is, on the other hand, by taking the trouble and incurring the risk, that the borrower makes his profits. All the profit which accrues from the average reproductive power of the capital belongs to its owner the lender. Any extra productiveness which the borrower can get out ·of it by attention, intelligence, or speculation, belongs to himself. It follows that the rate of interest in any community will keep very close to the rate of profit there attainable from the investment of capital directly by its owner.

It is very common to speak of the " price of money" when the rate of interest is meant, and to say that " the price of money should be regulated in the open market like that of any other commodity." The former phrase is as incorrect as to call rent the "price of land." The latter proposition is quite true if taken literally—that the actual price of coins and notes depends upon demand and supply—but it is a ·dangerous figure of speech when applied to interest. The idea meant to be conveyed—that interest is regulated by ·competition and by demand and supply—is however quite sound. It is as unjust to try to fix the rate of interest in any other way as it would be to fix the rent of land—and even more impossible to accomplish it. It is just as absurd to cry out against "usury," or the charging of interest on capital, as it would be to insist that every land owner should give his land to each applicant free of rent.

The old objection to "usury," based on the maxim "money does not beget money" arose from the misapprehension we have been combatting—that it was money that was really borrowed, and for the use of which interest was charged. If that were so, the maxim and the objection would both be sound. It is certain that one coin does not beget another, nor increase in value by use or hoarding. It would therefore be absurd to charge interest for the use of coins. If they were scarce people might be willing to pay a premium for the use of them, as they would for the use of any other tool. But such use would of necessity be momentary, confined to the one act of paying them away, and any recompense for it would consist of one payment, and not of a continuous rent. But it is certain on the other hand that capital *does* beget capital, and that no one will lend it without a continuous rent for its use. Those who speak of interest as being paid on money confound the conveyance with that which is conveyed. If a man lends seed wheat, he may require more bushels in return than he gave, as his share of the increase. And if the borrower takes the wheat home in a cart, he knows very well that the extra bushels he has agreed to pay are not rent for the cart, but for the wheat. Yet, if he takes home instead money to buy seed wheat, such money being the conveyance of the capital to be invested in the wheat, ten to one he will think that the interest charged is not for the wheat but for the money.

Now, is there any relation between the number of coins and notes, in a community and the amount of its capital (spare wealth), or the rent (interest) charged for the use of it?

Our last considerations show us that there is not. The amount of capital in a country certainly does not depend on the extent of its currency alone, any more than on the quantity of any other single commodity it possesses. The facility for conveying that capital from hand to hand, and investing it, does depend to some extent on the amount of currency, if there be no other machinery for conveying value. The rate of rent or interest charged for it has, however, no reference to the extent of the circulation. If there be not sufficient instruments for the lending of capital, less capital will be lent than might be if there were enough currency. It will in that case be hard to get loans. But the interest on such capital as *is* lent will depend on the profit derivable from the use of the capital, and not on the scarcity of tools for its conveyance. The latter fact will certainly not make capital more productive, or enable the borrower to pay higher interest for it. It will rather tend to induce the original owner to use his own capital, and may possibly reduce his profits. In this way alone can a general scarcity of currency affect the general rate of interest, and then by reducing it.

Of course, if a bank be allowed large powers for the issue of notes, it is quite possible that that bank may lend at a somewhat lower rate of interest, and why? Because those powers are permissions to float its paper—trade on its credit—"run its face"—to that extent. They are equivalent to turning a large part of its credit into available capital. As it has thus a large temporary supply of capital—or of credit which answers the same purpose—it may lend cheaply for a time. If all banks largely increased·their issue simultaneously, there might be a general fall in interest for these reasons. But it would come, not from the increase of the currency, but from the temporary increase of credit available for use as capital. Of course this would cease when the total issues reached the limit of demand for currency, and the surplus began to come back to the banks, because the banks could not force their credit beyond that limit. In the case of an issue of inconvertible currency the result is similar. At first the expansion of credit supplies an increase of *quasi* capital, which cheapens the rate of interest. When the expansion of credit ceases—that is when depreciation comes, and it is not longer possible to force circulation at a profit, this cheapening comes to an end. Indeed, as a matter of fact, we generally find high rates of interest coincident with highly inflated currencies—such high rates being partly intended to cover the increased risks of loss incidental to those currencies.

It is plain, then, that except when an increase of currency represents an actual increase of capital or credit available for lending, which could not have been made available in

any other way, and as long as the increase does not exceed
the limits of demand for currency *as* currency, that increase
will not lower the rate of interest. Neither does a scarcity
of currency—unless that scarcity be a sign of decreased
general wealth—increase it.

In this connection we must notice the tremendous
machinery available for the conveyance and lending of
capital, without resorting to the use of currency at all. The
most powerful engine of this kind is a bank. It may seem
strange, in a country where banks are the chief source of
currency, to speak of them as in any sense substitutes therefor, but such they really are. To understand how this is,
we must ask and answer the question, " What is a bank? "

The readiest answer in most minds will be—" It is an
institution that deals in money, just as a grocer deals in tea
and sugar." How incorrect this is in a literal sense we have
seen from our inquiry into the nature of what is borrowed
and lent. We have seen that that is capital and not money.
Using money in the sense of capital, the definition is partly
correct. A bank does deal in capital, but not in the sense of
buying and selling it. It borrows capital from one set of
customers, its depositors, and lends it to another set, whose
notes it discounts. It also lends its own capital or credit,
both in the form of bank notes and in other ways. It may
seem a loose expression to speak of credit as capital, but
such it really is to all intents and purposes. Credit is purchasing power, and, as such, capable of producing more
wealth.

When a man deposits a sum of money in a bank he
lends it that amount, subject to recall at pleasure.
The bank acknowledges its debt to him by an entry
to his credit on its books. When he wishes to make
a payment, he draws a cheque on the bank, payable to his
creditor. When the creditor accepts the cheque, he agrees
to take the bank for his debtor, instead of the man he has
dealt with. He may, or may not, actually touch the cash
called for by the cheque. He is very likely simply to deposit
it and get credit on the books, as we have already noticed in
speaking of London banking. Of course such a process is
just as available for lending as for paying debts. The borrower may be willing to take a cheque, and the consequent
credit at the bank instead of money ; and he may use all that

credit through cheques of his own making, without the with-
drawal of a single dollar from the bank. In the latter case
we see that a man may be a depositor, and use his whole deposit without a single dollar passing.

Again, when a man induces a banker to discount a note
for him, he exchanges his own obligation either for coin,
credit on the books, or bank notes, which are only another
form of obligation from the bank Except in the first case
there is an exchange of debt for debt—his debt against the
bank's. He borrows then from the bank. not money, even
in appearance, but the bank's credit which people will accept—on production of cheques or notes—instead of money.
In this case, as in the former, the whole transaction of borrowing and using capital may take place without the use
of a single dollar of money or other currency.

It is clear then that banks do not deal principally in money
in the proper sense. They handle a good deal of it, but not
as much in proportion to the business they do as retail grocers
or dry goods men, who sell chiefly for money. Their real
staple is capital, largely in the form of credit. They do not
even deal primarily in *currency* though their obligations pass
current for the same reasons as good private paper does—
though to a greater extent. The issue of currency is but an
accident of banking—a method of mobilizing its credit-
capital. In England, where banking is brought to its highest
perfection, only the Bank of England issues currency at all.

Are a bank's power of lending limited by the extent of the
general currency? Clearly not, since it can lend capital in
other forms. Are they limited by its own powers of issue ?
To some extent they are, for if it cannot issue notes, it must
refuse some customers who can only use notes, unless, or
until, it have a supply of other currency on hand. But in
regard to the general public, its powers of lending are limited
solely by the amount of resources it has to lend. What do
these consist of ? Paid-up capital and credit. Under the
latter head we include deposits, for as these are debts due
to depositors, they are advances on the credit of the bank.
If they have plenty of these resources, they can find ways
and means to lend them.

Perhaps the best proof of our assertion can be found in
the actual circumstances of our own country. If banks could
lend nothing but currency, they could lend no more at one
time than there was in the country at that time.

We find by a late *Gazette* that there were at the end of October, 1879, the following amounts of currency in circulation:—

Bank Notes............................		$23,201,000
Dominion Notes issued................	$12,642,000	
Less reserve held by banks, and not available for circulation............	8,707,000	
		3,935,000

Total Notes in circulation.................... $27,136,000

We have no such exact record of coin in circulation. Large amounts are held as reserves and, of course, cannot circulate. We know, however, that except for small change, there is very little coin in use. Perhaps, we will not be far wrong in calling the total currency, including all kinds of coin and notes, $28,000,000 in round numbers.

Now, what about loans? We find them stated as follows: Total loans to governments and to individuals

in round numbers.............................. $124,000,000

That is, the banks had out on loan at that time nearly 4½ times, in nominal value, the amount of the total circulating medium of the country. And this currency was at the same time serving the purpose of all other loans, made by other corporations and by individuals, as well as all the cash transactions of four millions of people. It is clear then that these banks did not lend money—the tool of exchange. If there were but 28 millions of bushels of wheat in Canada, the warehousemen could not lend 124 millions of bushels, besides suping the home consumption. What then did they lend? They lent these things :—

Paid up capital........................	$67,260,000	
Less amount held as reserves, and bank premises....................	18,210,000	
		say $49,000,000
Deposits by governments and individuals—that is loans on the banks' credit—in round numbers..............................		76,000,000
Total resources....................		$125,000,000

Or rather, as we, see they did not lend quite all of these, as they had to keep a certain amount disengaged for current demands. No better illustration could be given of the extent to which banking takes the place of currency, in the exchange of property and the lending of capital.

We say in the exchange of property, for most bank transactions arise from the sale of property by one person, and its ultimate purchase for use by some other, perhaps a third, fourth, or fifth party.

What shall we say then of the nature and uses of a bank after this consideration of what it does?

It is a corporation which deals in capital available for lending. It takes loans from depositors, lends this capital to those whose notes it discounts, and lends its own credit besides in the form of bank notes. It is to some extent a collecting agency. It is to a very large extent a medium of exchange. It handles a good deal of money, but only incidentally as any other trader might. So far from being a principal source of money, it is in a great degree a substitute for money. Its right to issue bank notes confers on it no power to create money or any kind of currency, unless these notes be made legal tender. Its issues rest on exactly the same foundation as good private promissory notes. This function is no essential part of banking, and is permitted only for the public convenience.

And what of the rate of interest charged by banks? Does that depend on the extent of their issues?

It depends on the resources (not only of banks but of all other lenders) which are available for loans, and the profit derivable from them. We have seen that the resources of the banks did not depend on the amount of currency. Neither did the resources of other lenders. Neither did the average rate of profit.

On what *did* this latter depend?

On the opportunities for productive investment and the supply of capital. Such opportunities are generally better in a new country than in an old one—in a thinly settled country than in one that is over-peopled—in "good times" than in "hard times"—when speculation is brisk, than when confidence is weak. It is then to be expected that at such times and in such countries, lenders will ask and borrowers will give, comparatively higher rates of interest.

This, we find, to be the case.   In England the rate is always lower than here—here it is lower than in Manitoba.   During the late depression the rate was low in the United States— in England some of the banks actually charged a premium for taking and holding deposits!   Why? Just because there was no investment open for the capital.   It seems then that a low rate of interest is by no means always a desirable symptom.   It may be, and often is, a sign of commercial depression and lack of enterprise.

Again, in England where the rate is low, there is a comparatively contracted circulation.   In the United States the rate was higher during the times of inflation than after resumption was agreed upon.   In Manitoba and other new countries, which, as we have seen, actually must and do have more currency for their business than older ones, the rate is very high.

From all this we can deduce the following propositions with certainty.

The amount of capital in a country has no relation whatever to the amount of currency.

The amount of capital *available for lending* may be increased to a certain extent by issues of paper currency, where there is not enough in circulation, because such issues mobilize a part of the capital, but this is only true where these issues do not exceed the demand for currency as a medium of exchange.   Consequently, in a country where the volume of currency is allowed to regulate itself, as here, according to the public demand, no permanent increase of available capital would result from a forced issue of paper.

The rate of interest bears no relation to the volume of currency.

If there be such a scarcity of currency as to interfere with the lending of capital, other substitutes will be used, or less will be lent.   In either case the rate of interest on what *is* lent, will be determined altogether by the average productiveness of investment.   No scarcity of available capital will raise the rate to a point above what could be made by the use of capital—it would simply prevent the use of capital in some instances.   No abundance of capital can lower it much, or permanently, below that point, for, if such a tendency appeared, capital would not be lent at all, but invested by its owners.

There is only one connection then in which the issue of currency has any bearing upon the accommodation of borrowers. We have already noted that certain trades require more currency than others, especially the produce trade. Now, the activity of these trades is periodical, varying with the seasons. At the brisk seasons, the dealers in those trades not only require more accommodation than usual, but require it chiefly in currency of some kind, since bank credit and cheques would not serve their purpose. If the banks, whose customers they are, could not supply them with increased loans in currency, their business would be hindered. It is then necessary, to prevent that inconvenience, that these banks should be able to make increased issues of notes at such times, as they could not hoard other currency for the purpose. This is of course no permament increase of the circulation, as it comes back again after the period of activity. Nor does its convenience show that a general increase in the volume of currency would make capital more plentiful. The need for it is not a need for more capital ; it is a need for the conversion of capital which the bank already possesses, and could lend in other forms, into the form best suited to the circumstances of certain traders. A general increase of currency – a new issue by the government for instance— would not give the same relief. If the general currency were increased, the banks would have to buy it with coin, or in some way exchange value for it before they could lend it, which is not what they want to do. It is not a general scarcity which troubles them, but a local one in their own offices. What they require, and what they have, is the power to cut up their credit into small negotiable debts— bank notes—and lend it directly in this form. This power is therefore, but a necessary part of the system of a free and open market for currency—a provision for allowing those who need capital, and can pay interest on it, to have it in the form which suits them.

CHAPTER VI.

"ABSOLUTE" OR "FIAT" MONEY.

A small school of "financiers" in Canada have been lately preaching the doctrine that intrinsic or commercial value is not a necessary quality of money—that a good currency may be made of articles that are not valuable in themselves, and are not promises to pay value. They urge that government should issue a paper currency, consisting of notes which are not acknowledgements of debt, but which are stamped with certain denominations of value—"$1.00," "$5.00," &c. This currency would be put in circulation by being paid out to the creditors of the government for value—to contractors, and laborers on public works for example. Of course it would have to be declared by law "legal tender." The basis of this theory is the doctrine that the law of legal tender confers value on any currency. We have discussed this question already and know that it cannot confer value on what is valueless without it, though it may give currency to coins or notes that are of very doubtful character, and would not circulate at all without such a law. If carried to its logical conclusion, such a doctrine would mean that the law could make a copper cent worth as much as a gold dollar. In fact it is a little too absurd to be declared in all its nakedness Our financiers therefore qualify it by a theory which we may call that of "incorporeal or vicarious value." This theory is that if Government issues pieces of paper, stamped as dollars and multiples of a dollar, and compels its creditors to take these in payment for labor and commodities, they acquire by the process a value equal to that for which they were exchanged. A favorite illustration is that if a laborer do a dollars worth of work for the Government, and get one of these dollar-tokens in payment, the token becomes thenceforth a real dollar. It is said to represent the days work which it cost, and it is argued that anything is worth what it cost to ob-

tain it. The same argument applies to the case of a con-
tractor who should furnish supplies and get "fiat" dollars
in payment.

Let us see where this theory would land us. Of course,
if simple exchange for value confers value on the currency
used, it can make no difference whether that currency be
issued by Government or by private parties. It follows
that counterfeiters wrong nobody. As soon as they have
"uttered" their brass dollars or pewter dimes—that is exchange them for value—the latter are as good as if they were
made of gold or silver. The taker is fully paid, since his
very acceptance confers the value he takes them at. Nay
more, the country is richer by the fact that new articles of
value have come into existence—new dollars and dimes as
good as the best—and of course money is a form of wealth.

It follows, further, that anybody could pay all he owes,
whether possessed of any property or not—if only his credi-
tory were intelligent enough to receive the new doctrine.
He has only to issue paper tokens for the number of dollars
required, and induce his creditors to accept them. Then
they will be paid in full, and there will be that much more
money in the country. Labor would be in great demand,
since everybody could get his work done, and pay the laborers fully and generously, without any cost to himself.
On second thoughts, however, it is not likely that any body
would care to work, since he could buy all he wanted without that trouble. It would be easier to make dollars than to
earn them. Any two men, one of whom possessed some
property to start with, might borrow a dollar stamp and sit
down to a day's solid business of buying and selling. Every
time the property changed hands each would be richer by
the value of it. How they would chuckle as the piles of
"vicarious" dollars grew at their elbows! Canada would
of course desert the old fashioned ways of agriculture and
commerce, and enrich herself by constant domestic exchange, till her wealth surpassed that of all the nations of
the world.

But it may be said that it requires the compulsion of law,
along with the exchange for value, to make paper tokens
dollars. Well then, why not declare by law that all such
paper tokens, and all counterfeit coins, *are* dollars, and compel every one to take them as such? The universal agreement

to take a currency embodied in such a law would of course
have the same effect on private as on national issues. "Oh,"
say our financiers, "the issue of currency is a prerogative and
duty of Government." In other words, if their theory be
true, it is a prerogative and duty of Government to prevent
the people from enjoying the tremendous source of wealth
which the newly discovered economic laws open to them.
They need never suffer lack of funds—there need be no
more poor in the land—all thoughts of toil, all ideas of giving value for value might be scattered to the winds—but "it
is the prerogative ánd duty of Government" to keep the
lamp of Aladdin that can accomplish all this to itself.

We see that the theory of "vicarious value" does not
greatly diminish the absurdity of the naked proposition.

A favorite name for this kind of currency is "absolute
money," a name which is evidently intended to mark some
intrinsic superiority in itself. The train of thought of our
financiers seems to be something like this. "The precious metals are commodities, and are therefore, though the
most constant in value of all commodities, yet subject to
more or less variation. Any currency consisting of these,
or promises to pay them, must be also variable—still more a
currency based on any other commodity. Let us have then
a 'money' whose usefulness does not depend on any
quality in itself which may be subject to variation—which
is based on nothing variable, but simply on the fiat of law
which makes it money. This will be money and nothing
else, 'absolute money,' just as pure spirit is 'absolute
alcohol.' Surely this will be invariable in value, and
subject to none of the vicissitudes of commodities. Its value
will be absolute like its nature."

Now what meaning can we attach to such expressions as
"absolute value" and "absolute money"? That which is
absolute has no relations with anything else. Absolute
space, absolute power, absolute knowledge are infinite, and
cannot be compared with any other space, power or knowledge. Absolute value too, can bear no relation to any other
value, and cannot be compared with the value of other
things, or be expressed in terms of any commodity.
A thing possessing only absolute value could not be said to
be worth so much of any other thing—it could have no exchange value whatever. Yet this latter is the only kind of

value which can be useful in an instrument of purchase or a standard of exchange. It follows that "absolute" money, possessing only "absolute" value, could bear no relation to the worth of any commodity—could not be brought at all into comparison with tangible things—and would be utterly useless either as a standard of exchange or an instrument of purchase. In fact, since money is a tool ·for those purposes, "absolute money" is a conception as absurd and impossible as that of an "absolute axe," possessed only of "absolute sharpness," and which could be brought into no relation with, and could produce no effect upon, a log of wood.

Yet the train of reasoning we have referred to is correct enough. Any money or currency possessing commercial value, is, and must be, subject to variations. The only invariable currency possible would be the one suggested. Its characteristic being an absolute negation of value, it would be as invariable as *zero*—always and invariably *worth nothing*.

It is very common in speeches and writings favoring the new currency, to find a glorification of "absolute money" followed by a contrast between "a currency based on one dear and limited commodity," (viz. gold), and one "based on all the assets and credit of the nation"—of course in favor of the latter. It is very possible that those who use such language do not see their inconsistency. It is more than probable that some of those whom they address may fancy that the two things so be-lauded are the same, or at least co-existent. Yet a currency based on national assets and credit must consist of promises to pay money or value—of notes payable on demand or in the future—while "absolute" or "fiat" money would consist of mere tokens. The two are as wide apart as the poles, and could not even exist together, since the poorer would inevitably drive the other out of use. It is necessary then to keep the two ideas of "fiat money" and a currency based on anything whatever, whether coin or credit, entirely distinct.

But it is said "a fiat dollar in the hands of a laborer on government works would be a proof that he has done a certain amount of work and a certificate of his right to be paid." Certainly it would—but who should pay him ? Under a law of legal tender, the first man who sold him any goods without a stipulation against "fiat" money would be com-

pelled to pay him, instead of the government for whom he
did the work. " But this man again could pass it off on
another." Perhaps he could, and so the burden of paying
for work the nation should have paid for would be shifted
from one shoulder to another. But unless the government
were bound in some way, and at some time, to redeem these
certificates of work done, the loss—the actual payment—
must ultimately fall on some individual, no matter how
often it may be shifted. This would be simple repudiation
of national obligations, and robbery of individuals. The notes
would not be currency at all, but orders on the first or last
taker to pay the nation's debts. If the government *were* so
bound, these certificates would be in effect ordinary inconvertible notes, with which we have already dealt, and all the
arguments about "absolute money " would have no reference
to them at all.

A popular argument for both inconvertible and fiat currencies is that they afford " cheap money." We have already
seen that they could not do so in the sense of reducing the
rate of interest, which is the idea meant to be conveyed. The
statement is however true in its literal sense, and is the most
complete condemnation of those currencies. Cheap things
are such as cost little or are worth little. "Fiat money "
would cost only the paper and printing, and be worth ultimately only that much. Inconvertible money costs only the
same amount at the time of issue, but is worth more. Still
it is cheap. When three greenback dollars were worth one
in gold, greenbacks were cheap money. When 288 francs
in *assignats* were worth one franc in gold, *assignats*
were extremely cheap money. Yet, in the end, each of those
greenbacks which were only worth $33\frac{1}{2}$ cents at the time
of issue has cost, or will cost, the country one dollar to redeem it. The same would have been true of *assignats* had
they not been repudiated. We see then that inconvertible
notes are cheap in the very worst sense—they are things of
small value which cost the price of more valuable ones.
Plainly they are not a desirable kind of cheap money—even
if any kind were so. But, since value is the quality by which
money does its work, cheapness is the worst fault it can have.
Even if cheap notes did not ultimately cost as much as gold
dollars, they would be inefficient in proportion to their cheapness. Cheap money is a thing of the same nature as a dull

axe or a weak steam engine, an instrument which fails in the very quality it should have in prefection. If these inferior tools cost as much as good ones, the parallel with inconvertible notes is complete.

It is sometimes urged, again, that "fiat" notes, though not money themselves, *represent* money, and therefore can fulfil all the functions of money. If they represented it in the same way that a bank note or cheque does—by constituting a title to money—this would be true to a certain extent. These can do most of the things that money can. But if "fiat" notes represent money in any intelligible way, it can only be in a pictorial sense. Will a picture of a dollar do the work of a dollar? It is just as reasonable to ask whether the picture of a cow will perform the functions of a cow. Can you milk it? Will it raise a calf? How much will the butcher give you for it? He might give you something for a chattel mortgage on a cow—but you must not think that both the mortgage and the picture represent the cow in the same sense.

A very entertaining advocate of "fiat" money in the Toronto press closes a glowing tribute to its worth by describing it as "never redeemable, but redeemed every hour and day." This is his poetic fashion of asserting that a "fiat" dollar would be redeemed every time it was accepted as payment for value—that it would in fact be redeemable in any commodity that could be bought with it. No doubt this is a pretty fancy, and highly creditable to the imagination of its author, but it is one which could hardly supply to the noteholder the place of real value of some kind in his currency. "Fiat" money might be redeemable and redeemed, by force of law, in different commodities, but it is as certain as a proposition of Euclid that it would be redeemed at a very small percentage of its face value—a percentage decreasing with every new issue of paper. It is also certain that such redemption as did take place would be effected at the expense of individuals, and not at the expense of the Government which had got the benefit of the issue.

But probably, after all, the advocates of the new currency would hardly be prepared to carry their theory fully into practice. It is necessary to adduce new and startling reasons for discarding gold and introducing paper—for substituting the negative value of zero for the positive value of some

5

actual commodity. Yet it seems from their publicly an-
nounced programme, that they do not propose to base
the new currency solely on the miraculous transmutation
worked by a " fiat." They would make provisions, indeed,
which might give it a certain value by the operation of ordinary mundane laws. Whether this inconsistency be due
to some doubts of their own theory, or be only a concession
to the weaker brethren, we cannot say. Their platform, as
settled at a meeting of the leaders in Toronto is in substance
as follows :

Government should issue, in payment of all expenses,
" fiat " or token dollars, not being promises to pay—should
make these legal tender, and abolish all bank issues. These
notes would be receivable by government in payment for
crown lands, and the sums so received would be applied to
the reduction of the national debt. They would also be
exchangeable, in certain sums, for three per cent perpetual
bonds like the English consols. We gather, from other
utterances, that they would also be receivable for all dues
payable to government.

Now it is evident that this exchangeability for land, and
receivability for debts due to government, would give some
value to the new issues as securities, whether it would make
them a good currency or not. But would the value be considerable ? We think not. If the whole amount of the
currency were only equal to the debts owing to government
by citizens, and if this were the only currency, and not in
excess of the requirements for currency purposes, it might
be at par. Any kind of currency, whether notes or tokens,
which is made receivable by the government is, in effect if not
in form, an acknowledgement of debts due by them. In re-
ceiving it for dues they simply honour their obligations,made
to the persons who first took the notes for value. Under
the circumstances mentioned, a fiat currency would be a
security as valuable as gold, since every dollar of it could be
used, at its face value, to meet debts which would otherwise
require gold to meet them. The government, too, would
stand just in the same position as if it had issued demand
notes, since by taking these notes instead of gold it would
be in effect cashing them in that money. For instance, if a
government issued $20,000,000 of fiat money in any
year, as the only currency of the country, and had to

receive that amount from its own citizens for dues, it would simply get back the notes it had issued—would in fact only cancel those debts which had been created by the issue of the notes Under these circumstances the issue of such currency woud simply be a means of setting off the nation's revenue against its expenses. It would have succeeded in deferring payment only for a year, or for whatever shorter times the notes had remained in circulation. Now the essential advantage claimed for a fiat currency or one of greenbacks, as far as concerns the government, is that they would both *indefinitely* defer payment. "It might re-issue those notes" you may say. True, and so it might issue new ones. Its capacity of issuing is in no respect increased by the return of its former paper. The whole transaction is just the same as if an employer of labor, who also kept a shop at which his laborers dealt, should issue to them certificates of the amount he owed them for work, and take these again in payment of subsequent debts to himself. If he issued no more than these subsequent debts required, his certificates would be worth their face value to all who owed him money. If he issued beyond this point, the balance would be worth nothing unless they contained a contract to pay the holder in cash. Now fiat notes would contain no such contract, and therefore any surplus over the amount owing to government would be worthless.

Although, in the circumstances we have stated, this issue would have a certain value as a *security*, it would have one defect fatal to its usefulness as a currency. A permanent currency must be one that can continue in circulation without injury to its value, or one that is convertible into something else that will take its place in circulation. Now these issues of token dollars would derive all their value from the fact that government would take them in payment of debts. As soon as they were paid in they would go out of circulation, and would not be replaced by anything else. Each one might be worth as much, *as a security*, as a bank note. But as soon as its owner cashed it, by paying it on a debt, it would go out of existence—while a redeemed bank note is replaced in circulation by the gold that is given for it. Token dollars, therefore, whatever their value as securities, would not constitute a permanent currency at all.

But of course such an arrangement would destroy all the

advantages claimed for the new currency. One of these is
that it would furnish a means of borrowing from our own
people, instead of on debentures sold abroad, the funds required for public works, such as the Pacific Railway, which
we could not meet out of revenue even if all imposts were
retained. In this case they would have to be made non-
receivable on dues, as current revenue would be required to·
meet ordinary expenses. We should consequently have, each
year, an addition to the total circulation equal to the amount
spent on such works. Now as such works are an inevitable
burden on all nations, and especially on Canada--since in fact
it is chiefly to carry on such works that the new currency is
proposed—it is just as inevitable that we should have to issue
more than the commercial exchanges required, and therefore
the whole currency would be worthless.

It may be argued that convertibility into land and bonds
would avert this danger. But we have seen, when treating
of the old French currency, that only such notes as were not
required for circulation could be so converted, and these only
when held in large quantities by individuals. Notes needed
for the exchange of goods could not be invested in Manitoba
lands, neither could the few dollars of savings held by some
laborer. We have seen too that the number of notes required for circulation rises with the largely increased issue.
so that there is always a cry for more currency soon after a
period of inflation. The surplus capable of being so redeemed or converted would therefore always be very small.
Moreover, as crown lands are sold at a fixed price per acre,
each dollar would represent a certain quantity of land,
though not in any certain locality. Its value then, even if
available for conversion into land, would depend on that of
the piece of land for which it was exchangeable. Now, as
this would be absolutely unascertainable with any certainty,
the value of the notes as security would be a pure question
of speculation.

Nor would their actual conversion, even in large quantities, permanently decrease the volume of currency. What
could Government do with them? They would be of no use
to it unless issued again for value. Our theorists say, " apply
them on the national debt." To do this, they must be sold
for gold, and sold in Canada, as they would not be current
elsewhere. In any case it will be seen they must come again
into circulation.

It is worth noticing too, that as soon as any depreciation took place, Government would have to issue a proportionately larger amount each time, and so progressively exaggerate the inflation.

Convertibility into bonds would not give any more help. The same arguments which apply to land, apply to these also. Besides, the bonds would not be payable at all, and the interest only in paper. Nobody would choose them as an investment in ordinary times. Nobody would seek them as a means of converting his currency into anything more stable, as they would be themselves based on the currency.

In short, as before stated, no kind of convertibility will save a currency from depreciation, or make it a permanent currency at all, except convertibility into something which can also be used as currency, and which will be generally recognized as solid and trangible money, possessing intrinsic value. That is, no convertibility into any other kind of security except demand notes, or into any other commodity except the precious metals, will save it. Even a greenback currency which holds out the prospect of payment in coin, sometime in the future, is stronger than one convertible into land, and into that alone. Experience is the best proof of this, and the most striking experience is that of France already given in detail. *Assignats* were not only convertible into land, but were actual mortgages on land, and bore a daily interest. *Mandats* were titles to the actual possession of land without form of foreclosure, and both were convertible into bonds. The lands mortgaged were not wild lands, but the choicest in France, and the issue was kept down to the estimated value of the lands. The holder of *mandats* might take possession of any city or country property of the nation not occupied already to their face value. He would not have to make a toilsome journey into the wilderness to select his property, or separate himself from civilization and old associations to enjoy it. Yet the sales of these lands were comparatively few—certainly not more than if they had been offered in the ordinary way—probably not nearly so many. And what was worse, both *assignats*, and the *mandats* which followed them, fell to a point only paralelled by the worthless currency of the Confederate States of America. This mortgage-currency, "land-money" as its friends called it, was more utterly depreciated than any unsecured inconvertible currency of modern times,

with perhaps the exception named. Its value might be expressed in our currency by saying that a franc note stood
compared with a franc coin as *one cent* to $2.88. Where then
might a currency, whose value rested on convertibility by
purchase into unknown wild lands in the North-West, be
expected to stop in its downward course ?

Let us now briefly review what we have ascertained about
the proposed national currency of "absolute money."

By proposing to make it legal tender on debts due to the
government, its advocates have practically given up all the
arguments in favor of a currency which depends for its value
on nothing except the fiat of law. For we have seen that a
fiat currency receivable by the government on dues is of the
nature of demand notes, redeemable in value of some kind,
up to the amount to which it could be redeemed by payment on such dues. It would, when a surplus existed, be.
weaker than an ordinary greenback currency however, since
the latter contains pledges to pay sometime, while the fiat
currency would not ; and any value it might have would
arise from the hope that the surplus might some day disappear, and afford a chance of its redemption. This hope we
have seen must prove illusory if the fiat currency be used to
furnish funds for new and extensive public works. Indeed
as soon as the operation of the currency was understood, such
a hope would cease to be entertained, and the value of the
fiat notes would vanish with it. It would therefore derive
no permanent value, if issued beyond the limit referred to,
from its receivability on dues.

We have seen that convertibility into lands or bonds
would not help it. Its only basis then must be the power of
the fiat. We know from observation, as well as theory, that
this fiat is not of itself able to keep up the value of an inconvertible currency consisting of promises to pay. Such currencies always depreciate if not sustained by most exceptional
circumstances, and *one* case of depreciation would be quite
sufficient to show that a fiat cannot prevent their doing so.
Now, if a fiat cannot keep up the value of national promises
to pay, possessing real value as securities, it can still less
keep up the value of a currency which is worth nothing
apart from the fiat itself.

It is clear, then, that the proposed currency would be
vastly more liable to depreciation than inconvertible notes—

would not be likely in fact to retain any appreciable value whatever.

What other advantages are claimed for it as an offset to this tremendous defect?

Perhaps the chief of them is that it would afford a cheap method of paying for public works and would avoid the necessity of borrowing abroad. How could it do this? " By the repeated issue of notes whenever required," we are told. But as soon as the issue exceeded the demand for currency, even if not before, the notes would depreciate very rapidly. Each issue that came out would have to be larger than the last—the depreciation would be hastened—and the receipts of the government for its obligations would proportionately diminish. In course of time the notes would be as practically worthless as the French *assignats*. and when they reached anything like that point government would have to stop issuing.

Could they be used in paying public debts already contracted? Certainly not by actually sending them abroad, as they would not be current there. Neither could they be so applied by converting them into gold at home, for the supply of gold would not be greater, or the price of it less, after their issue. The process of buying gold for transmission abroad, with a depreciated currency, will hardly be considered a desirable mode of paying debts.

Take a historical illustration for both cases. The United States greenbacks were certainly more likely to be valuable than a fiat currency. Did their issue avert the necessity of borrowing for the carrying on of public business? Was it not rather true that the public debt was more rapidly increased during the time of their issue than ever before? It may be said the war caused this. But is not the exceptional expenditure of a war just one of those emergencies which a greenback currency would meet, if it could do all that is claimed?

It is urged that this currency would make capital more plentiful, assist in the development of our resources, and reduce the rate of interest. It is said too that the occurrence of hard times is evidence of a scarcity of currency in the country, and that an increased supply of the latter would avert them for the future. We have already shown the absurdity of the first contention, unless it be true that the country has not as much currency as is required to mobilize its capital—for this is all that currency can do.

In regard to the second allegation, we have yet had no proof that any person who has had capital has found any difficulty during the hard times in obtaining currency for it, or has had to resort to barter in making purchases. The real trouble was a lack of capital, not of the means of moving or exchanging it. But it is said "many a man had commodities to sell, for which he could not get money." Very true, but that was due to lack of demand, not to lack of coins and notes to buy with. The depression of the lumber trade, for instance, arose from the slackening of building operations the world over, and not from any lack of currency. No buyer who came here, able and willing to invest in lumber, was prevented from doing so for lack of bank notes. No grain buyer ever pretended that he gave low prices for wheat because he could not get as many bank notes as he could give security for to the banks. But the best proof of this lies in the fact that we have a free and open currency market in Canada, within certain limits, and that the demand for currency does not nearly approach those limits. The banks have authority to issue notes up to the amount of their paid-up capital, and are only too glad to do so when they can. Yet all the banks in Canada, with the power of issuing over $60,000,000 in notes, had in circulation in the height of the autumn produce trade only about $23,000,000 in paper. That is, they could only dispose of about one-quarter of the amount they were authorized by law to sell.

But our financiers say " People had to buy or borrow this currency, give value for it, or pay interest on it." Certainly, they had to buy it, or pay interest on the capital it conveyed. And could the new currency be otherwise obtained ? We trow not. The government would not give it away. The banks would not lend capital, in that particular form of all others, without interest. In so far as it embodied a real extension of capital or credit, it would of course extend the amount of funds available for investment; but we have seen that it could not be such an embodiment if issued beyond the needs of circulation. This extended capital, and this new currency, could only come into the possession of the needy in the same way as before, by purchase or borrowing on interest. If the currency of Canada be to-day, as appears from the bank returns, as large as people will buy and use, no permanent increase of capital or reduction of interest could follow the issue of a larger supply.

The only means of realizing the prospect of an unlimited supply of capital in the form of currency which our theorists hold out to us, possessing any appearance of plausibility, would be to allow private individuals to issue notes, and make them legal tender. Then of course every man, rich and poor, could issue obligations or tokens to be used as currency, and compel their acceptance by the public. This is the only state of things to which their glowing descriptions of a general plethora of capital could apply, and we fear even this kind of currency would be open to some danger of depreciation!

To state the case briefly; currency is only useful to mobilize capital, consisting either of credit, or commodities already in existence. If there is not enough to do this, more is needed. If there is enough for this purpose, no increase of the currency can augment the amount of capital in existence. How much is enough can only be determined by leaving the market open to currency users to buy as much as they need.

. Finally, as to Canada, it appears that we *have* an open currency market, in which the demand for currency only equals about one quarter of the available supply. Therefore we have currency enough in Canada, and a further issue could in no way help us. As we have seen that it could in many ways injure us, we conclude that any action in that direction would prove an unmitigated misfortune.

The proposed currency would certainly bring with it, not only the economic disasters inseparable from inconvertible issues, but also the social and political demoralization that are the natural outcome of the "obliteration of thrift." If the government set the example of living wholly on its credit, and forcing all creditors to wait its own time for payment, still more, if, as proposed, it should shift all domestic debts from its own shoulders to those of individuals by means of "fiat money," private parties would try to follow its example. When it is once established as a principle of public morality that a nation need never do more than acknowledge its obligations on paper, without providing for their payment at any future time, it will be hard to hold private debtors to a strict account. Micawber used to feel

that all claims against him were discharged as soon as he
had given his note of hand for the amount. How he would
have revelled in the delights of a system under which a
simple token of the amount due would be sufficient, without
signature or stamps! For he would surely reason that if this
mode of payment on the part of a nation was honest, it would
be as honest on the part of a Micawber.

Extravagance would of course be fostered in all ranks by the
theory that it costs nothing to spend freely. Sir John Mande-
ville, who visited Tartary in 1322, gives full expression to the
modern theory. He says: "The Emperour may dispenden
als moche as he wile with outen estymacioun. For he
despendeth not, ne maketh, no money, but of lether emprented, or of papyre. * * * For there, and beyonde
hem, thei make no money nouther of gold nor of sylver.
And therefore he may dispende ynow and outrageously."
Truly there is nothing new under the sun, even in theories of
currency! And there can be no doubt that a government
now-a-days, authorized to make money of "lether emprented or of papyre," would follow the example of the great
Khan, and spend "ynow and outrageously, withouten
estymacioun." No doubt too the same result would follow.
We read that this Tartar original of the "fiat money" plagiarism fell to a very smll fraction of its nominal value, caused
great discontent and misery, and was finally abolished in
the 16th century, never to appear again. The Tartars are
therefore more than three centuries in advance of their
modern imitators. It is that length of time since they learned
that "papyre emprented" will not make good money.

CHAPTER VII.

OBJECTIONS TO OUR PRESENT CURRENCY.

It may be as well to notice separately some of the objections
made by the new Tartars to our present currency.

They say for example that, as we do not produce gold, we
have to borrow that which is used as bank reserves, and
which under their new system might be dispensed with, at
high interest, or buy it with our own productions. The latter

they assume we cannot do when the balance of trade is against us, as it generally is.

This is a palpable absurdity, except the statement that we buy our gold. That is the way we get it, and we buy it with our produce just as we buy iron or flannel, whether the balance of trade be for or against us. When it is against us no doubt some gold is re-exported, but the trade returns show that only a small fraction of the apparent difference between exports and imports goes in this way. No man or nation borrows gold *as* gold. A part of our borrowings may be turned into gold, just as the greater part is turned into material for public works, and no more interest is paid for one than the other. How could we ever buy such material abroad except by getting credit for it, as we now do, or by sending our produce in exchange for it? Fiat notes would never pass current for steel rails in Staffordshire.

It is again urged as an absurdity that our currency should be nominally based on gold, while only a small proportion of the amount of circulation is held as a reserve against it. But, as a matter of fact, it is not the gold held in reserve that guarantees the value of bank notes or government notes. It is the credit of the issuer, his ability to produce gold for the whole of the notes if necessary. It is the whole assets of the issuer, in fact, that constitute the real security. The reserve is intended only to meet the small percentage of notes likely to be presented for gold from time to time in the course of trade, and not to cover the whole issue. It is the ready cash of the bank or government, and not their whole resources. In the case of governments, the assets are generally indefinitely greater than the issue. In the case of our banks, they consist of the paid-up capital, notes discounted (less the amount due depositors) and the double liability of shareholders. At present (October, 1879) these may be put in round numbers as follows:—

Paid-up capital		$67,000,000
Double liability		67,000,000
Discounts	$124,000,000	
Less deposits	76,000,000	
		48,000,000
		$182,000,000
To cover in bank notes		23,000,000
Surplus		$159,000,000

Of course there are other minor liabilities, and there may be bad debts among the discounts, but the surplus is large enough to cover a great many such. It is the knowledge of this surplus capital available for the ultimate, if not immediate, cashing of notes which keeps up the value of bank issues. It is however necessary, to avoid temporary loss and inconvenience, that considerable reserves in gold should be held, of which more anon.

Another brilliant objection is, that, as bank notes are only acknowledgements of debt, and are lent for use in productive investments, the banks of Canada draw from labor a yearly tax of about $1,800,000 as interest on their own indebtedness! This is calculated at the rate of ten per cent. on an assumed circulation of $18,000,000, and is said to be a tax on the many for the benefit of the few. Now, as we already know, banks charge no interest whatever for the use of their notes *as currency ;* they charge it for the use of the capital or purchasing power conveyed by those notes. And why do the notes possess purchasing power ? Simply because they *are* debts, debts that everyone believes to be good, and is therefore willing to take instead of money. The bank's debt to the borrower, acknowledged by the notes, enables him to buy as much as he could buy with an equal nominal value in gold, wheat, or land. It is *credit* then on which the banks collect a "tax" from borrowers. And why should not the latter pay a "tax" for the use of capital in the form of credit, just as much as if he borrowed it in coin, grain or real estate ? A "tax" too is an impost levied by authority. Interest is a payment made by agreement, an agreement which no one will enter into unless he expects to profit by the transaction. Moreover, unless it is proposed to give private parties the right of issuing legal tender notes, the same complaint could be made against the nation under a system of "fiat" or inconvertible currency. The nation's notes would also be debts, which people who could not buy them would have to borrow and pay interest for.

But perhaps the most peculiar complaint of all, though a mere plagiarism from the 18th century inflationists of France, is that a gold-based currency will be taken by foreigners, and that consequently it is liable to leave the country at times ! This is true enough, though of course notes would come back. It really denotes a peculiar mental state

in a man when we find him complaining that an instrument
is too perfectly adapted to its uses ! Money is a tool to buy
with ; axes are tools to chop with. If our money is good of
its kind it will buy abroad as well as at home. If our axes
are good they will chop in any country to which they may
be taken. Yet we hear no one objecting to sharp axes of
good temper, because foreigners may like them and create a
"drain of axes from the country." The cry for money that
will only buy in Canada is as absurd as a cry for axes that
would lose their edge the moment they crossed the lines.

Perhaps some of these absurdities may seem too crude to
deserve notice, but they are all taken from the repeated utterances of Canadian advocates of "fiat" currency, either in
speeches or through the press. Nothing is too absurd to
reply to which is persistently urged upon the people by those
whom they consider as authorities.

CHAPTER VIII.

WHAT IS THE BEST CURRENCY FOR CANADA?

We have so far been chiefly occupied in discussing general
principles—in trying to understand the nature of money and
currency in general. It is now time to consider whether we
can make any useful application of these principles and this
knowledge, in determining what currency is best suited to
our own circumstances.

Those who have followed us hitherto will no doubt agree
on certain prime requisites that must belong to every sound
currency· It must consist either of articles possessing intrinsic value—of which metallic coin is the best example--
or of paper promises to pay such articles, and which possess
a value derived from the general belief that the debt they
acknowledge will be paid. Of course, promises to pay in
land or any valuable commodity would possess a certain
derived value as securities ; but, as we have seen, no notes
form a useful currency which are not promises to pay some-

thing equally available as a medium of exchange. Now the
only commodity practically available for that purpose is coin.
And, as we have also seen that promises to pay at some
indefinite time invariably depreciate, we may lay down the
general proposition that the only admissible paper currency
is one consisting of promises to pay coin on demand.

Although, if a paper currency possesses public confidence,
the calls for coin will be small, it follows from the existence
of any demand for it, that a sound paper currency cannot
exist alone. No matter how high may be the credit of the
issuer, if he be not prepared to give coin for such notes as
the holders wish to exchange for it, the currency will depreciate.

A currency of coin can of course exist alone. Our choice
then of a sound currency lies between one composed altogether of coin, and one composed of coin and demand notes
jointly.

There can be no hesitation in making the choice. No one
will deny that coin has been found to be too clumsy and inconvenient as a medium of exchange for every day transactions, especially in large amounts.

Should we have gold coin alone as the standard of value,
or is the "double standard" of gold and silver preferable?

If one metal alone be chosen as the standard, there is a
general admission that gold, as being the most precious
metal available in considerable quantities, and the most
constant in value, is the best for that purpose,. The only
question is whether we should not adopt both silver and
gold, and consider them as having an absolutely fixed value
relative to each other, and as varying equally with regard to
other commodities. The great objection to such a course is,
that this supposed fixity of relative value can never be anything but an assumption or legal fiction. The vicissitudes
of supply and demand which regulate the value of the two
metals affect them in different degrees. It may easily happen
that one grows more plentiful as the other grows rarer. It
is happening at present that the supply of silver increases
much more rapidly than that of gold. As a matter of fact
then, a double standard involves the use of two measures of
value assumed to be equal, but which are really unequal,
and of varying inequality at that. The consequence is,
either that the public is liable to deception in the use of these

measures, or that it actually disregards the fiction of law, by calculating values in one of the two standards to the exclusion of the other.

The latter is what usually happens The metal which the law rates relatively too high passes current with difficulty, or at a discount, especially in foreign exchanges. It is also sought for by those who have to make payments to the government, because they can buy it at its real value and pay it in at the value the law sets upon it, thus making a profit. This is now occurring in the United States, where it is found practically impossible to keep the new silver coinage in circulation. Coining is continued as the law requires, but the silver comes rapidly back after its first issue, so that the stock of it held by the Treasury is constantly increasing. As this coined silver left in the vaults represents capital lying idle, the loss to the government is very considerable. Of course, if silver were rated too low by law, the reverse of this process would take place--silver would flow out and gold in. As the relative values of the two do not remain long constant, no re-adjustment of the legal valuation could permanently prevent the wasteful accumulation of one or the other in the hands of government.

These are by no means all the evils of a double standard, but we think they are quite sufficient to lead us to reject the principle. They are the same in kind, though less in degree, as those which attend the attempt to give a greater value by law to paper currency than it would bear in the open market. As one of the two metals will always be overvalued, the principle inevitably lands us in that state of uncertainty as to the value of the currency which is the worst fault it can possess.

Our "best currency" then must have gold coin as its standard of value. Does this involve the purchase and retention, as unused capital, of large quantities of that coin. Reserves must be kept, but not necessarily large ones. As we have said before, while holders of paper know that they can get gold for their notes, they are content to keep the notes, which are more convenient for ordinary use, except when they want gold for use abroad. The percentage required for meeting the latter demand is not large. The greater the security offered for the ultimate redemption of notes, the less will be the risk of calls for gold. If the security be considered perfect, these calls will be limited strictly to those purposes for which nothing but gold will answer. We shall have occasion to discuss, later, whether certain improvements on our present system might not largely reduce the percentage now considered necessary as a reserve.

But it must not be forgotten that even the reserve so held is not dead capital. Every dollar of it is represented by notes which take its place in circulation. The banks do not suffer a direct loss of interest on the value they have invested in it. They simply forego some profits they might have made if they were not required to make that investment at all, but could base their circulation on credit alone.

This leads us to consider whether the credit of banks is the strongest possible basis for a paper currency, and whether, if it be not, the substitution of any other would be advisable in Canada.

The figures we have already quoted in regard to the circulation and resources of our banks would seem to show that the latter are amply sufficient, in the aggregate, to ultimately cover all possible demands of note holders. But when we consider the peculiarly sensitive nature of bank credit, and the contingencies which may lead to the bankruptcy of any individual institution, we can see that there is a real danger of injury to portions of our circulation.

The conditions of a bank's continued solvency are somewhat peculiar. Not only does it incur the usual risks of loss in business, but it becomes practically insolvent from the moment it has to refuse payment in gold for any of its notes. How powerfully this latter risk may operate in closing its career is easily seen.

A bank only keeps in reserve as much gold as it finds to be necessary for meeting ordinary calls. The rest of its capital is invested in a shape not immediately convertible into gold. All goes smoothly enough till some loss or temporary embarrassment becomes known to the public. A rumour starts at once that the "bank is shaky." Depositors are a timid race, and as soon as such a rumor, well founded or not, gains currency a " run " of greater or smaller extent begins. The bank is then suddenly called upon to refund the loans made to it by these depositors. This of itself is often a sufficiently heavy trial, but it is not all. The fact of a " run " being in progress, especially if it be known that the bank is hard pressed, alarms note holders as well. These also rush in to cash their securities while there is yet time. The bank must then not only repay what it owes, but repay it in a certain form, viz : gold. This sudden and double call for the repayment of nearly all its obligations to the public is often enough to exhaust the ready cash of an institution which is in a perfectly solvent condition if it only had time to realize its assets. It is especially likely to do so if rival banks join in the attack by presenting the large quantities of its notes they generally hold. As soon as this ready cash is exhausted the bank must close its doors, and go into liquidation for the benefit of those creditors who are still unsatisfied. It is obvious that such a sudden plunge into insolvency, with the consequent necessity of immediate realization, must greatly lessen the actual value of its assets, and may lead to considerable loss on the part of note holders and depositors, not to mention the heavy drain on those who own the bank's shares. But even where the assets so hurriedly brought into the market suffice ultimately to meet all debts, there is always a loss to such note holders as cannot afford to wait for the end of the liquidation before cashing their claims. As soon as a bank suspends payment its notes are quoted at a discount, and every one who is compelled to use them without delay loses that percentage. Now it happens that the very class who are forced to use their notes at once comprises those who can least afford such a loss. Men of capital can generally wait, and obtain the greatest possible dividend. It follows that any bank suspension necessarily involves considerable loss to the poorer note holders, no matter what may be the final result of the liquidation. This is a very serious evil and should have a remedy.

It is thought by some that it would be sufficient to make the note circulation a first lien on all assets of the bank. This would certainly be a just provision of law, since the takers of notes are not supposed to exercise the same discretion as the depositor, who deliberately makes choice of the bank which he is willing to trust. Yet we doubt whether it would be a perfect solution of the problem. It remains to be seen whether the confidence in the ultimate payment of notes which it would create would be sufficient to induce the public generally to take them at par, after the suspension of a bank. This is what should be aimed at, if banks are to

6

be allowed to issue at all. Provision should be made for maintaining the absolute security of note holders, no matter what disasters may over take the issuer.

There are several means of securing this end which we may now proceed to consider.

Perhaps the most obvious is to insist upon the banks holding in reserve a dollar in gold for every dollar of their circulation, this reserve to be liable for no other debts except the notes. This would no doubt be effective, but it would be rather cramping to the powers of the banks, who require to make occasional issues in excess of the average amount. There are seasons of the year, when the produce trade is brisk for example, at which a sudden and considerable increase of currency is required. This the banks could hardly furnish if they were compelled to procure an equal amount of gold before issuing it. In general, and at all times of the year, such a provision would nullify many of the advantages of paper currency, by requiring that the assets held against the notes should be held in the particular form prescribed, i.e. gold, instead of the form that might be most convenient to the banks. We may therefore decide that on the whole this is not a desirable arrangement.

Another plan is to allow the banks to issue a certain amount in notes, well below the figure of their assets, without holding any reserve, but to require dollar for dollar above that amount. This is the arrangement under which the Bank of England is allowed to issue. Its notes do not require to be covered up to the amount of about £15,000,000 ; but above that figure a sovereign must be deposited with the Government for each pound's worth of notes. So well does it work, under the circumstances of that country, that, in the worst crises that have occurred in the last thirty years, hardly a note has been presented for which the gold was not ready in the hands of the government. That is, the £15,000,000, to meet which the bank would have had to withdraw funds from other investments, has not been encroached upon. We need not say that it has also maintained the credit of the notes at the highest point. No doubt the fact that the uncovered amount approximately represents a debt owing to the bank from the government when the arrangement was made, and held in the form of consols which are thought to constitute a reserve against the notes, has something to do with the latter result. People seem to think that *all* the notes are thus practically secured Yet some authorities hold that the law gives no first lien on these consols, and the point has never been decided.

There is no reason why such a plan should not provide absolute security everywhere, if the limits of issue on credit were as nicely adjusted to the bank's circumstances as in this case. The only objection to it here would be the same as to. the last, though in a less degree, namely the lack of elasticity. This is not felt in England, where so much less currency in proportion to business is required, and where there are no periodical demands for more notes, in uncertain amounts.

Another plan, which has been tried and found effective, is that on which the National Bank system of the United States is based. A bank which asks power to issue notes must buy government securities to the amount of its proposed issue. It receives the interest on these, and, they are held as a special reserve against the notes. According to a late report of Mr. Knox, Comptroller of the Currency, there were 2000 national banks, whose total active issue was $302,000,000, secured by deposits of government bonds to the gold value of $349,000,090. Directly a bank fails, its deposit becomes pledged to the payment of its notes. Accordingly, though 69 national banks have failed since 1863, no one has lost a dollar by their notes. Of course, as these notes were payable in legal tender, they varied with the price of greenbacks before resumption, but no note holder sustained any loss through the failures of the banks. They were as good after as before.

A somewhat similar system is in force in the little kingdom of Man, where a practically independent " Home Rule " government exists. The only difference is that, instead of Government bonds, a deposit of mortgages on real estate is required, which bear interest there at about 4½ per cent. This deposit must cover, not only notes in circulation, but all those signed and held ready for issue. A most remarkable instance of its effective working has lately occurred. The Bank of Mona, doing business in the island, was a branch of the City of Glasgow Bank, whose failure has excited so much comment. Of course it suspended payment along with the parent institution—while its notes not only continued good, but were sought for as ivestments. The latter fact arose from the provision of law that the notes of a suspended bank shall bear interest at the legal rate of 6 per cent, till the securities held against them can be realized.

In both these plans we find again the same want of elasticity which our bankers tell us—and with reason —would be so great a fault in a Canadian system of issue by banks, although the prime requisite of security is supplied.

It yet remains to consider the case where the Government issues convertible paper itself, whether as the sole currency or in addition to bank issues. We are familiar with the latter state of things in Canada, since the Dominion Government claims the exclusive right to issue notes of certain very small and very large denominations, while it also issues others of the same denominations as bank notes. The large notes, and those of competing denominations, are chiefly held as reserves by the banks instead of gold, as they are " legal tender " in payment of their own notes.

Now there can be no doubt of the security of our present issue of notes, and there would be no doubt of it even if it became the sole currency, and were increased to the amount which the public at present require. There could be no danger, either, of a permanent over supply or depreciation, since any surplus currency would be converted at once into gold which is very easily got rid of. Any objection to the issue of Government demand notes as our sole currency must therefore be sought in other directions, and indeed they are not wanting

The first and most obvious practical difficulty is in the existence of so many banks having the right to issue under their charters. This profitable right could not of course be taken away—even when the old charters expired—without compensation. The process of extinguishing private issues all round would therefore be tedious and costly. This however would be sanctioned by the public if it were seen that counter-balancing advantages would result—but in that case only.

Now, what dangers would there be in the new system to set against its undoubted security ?

First, and greatest, would be the danger of extravagance on the part of the government. The power of issuing currency at will for the construction of new works, or to meet temporary embarrassments or deficits, would prove a heavy

temptation to any cabinet. They would be apt frequently
to forget, under pressure of difficulties or in face of demands
for new undertakings, that an issue of notes only deferred,and
did not cancel, the obligation to pay cash.   The result would
be a temporary over-supply of paper, the effects of which
would be more injurious to the Government than to trade.
Its character as convertible currency would make it good
enough, but could not keep it in circulation.   It would, in
fact, drive the surplus out of circulation. This surplus would
come in to the Government, through the banks, calling for its
face value in gold.   Consequently every issue over and above
the wants of circulation would involve a speedy demand
upon the nation for the immediate payment of the extra
amount.   It will be seen that while the power of unlimited
issue is likely to tempt a Government to trade too largely on
its credit, a convertible currency makes the credit given very
short, and its use is apt to lead to sudden and embarrassing
calls for cash when least expected.   It is probable, therefore, that it would be cheaper and safer to borrow the sum
required at once, at home or abroad,after due legislative delib-
eration, than to trust any Cabinet with the power of making
short forced loans without interest.

It is not unworthy of notice here that such a power would
give an outgoing Government a tremendous faculty of embarrassing their successors.

On the other hand, the limitation of the power of issue to
a certain amount would deprive the plan of much of its at-
tractiveness.

There is still another danger, apart from that of over-issue
in amount.   It concerns the nature of the uses to which the
funds obtained might be put.   We often find nations borrowing money to expend on public works that are either totally
useless, or at least, unproductive of revenue.   Under the last
head we may think of our own Intercolonial and Pacific
Railways.   Of course, all expenditures of this kind create a
heavy permanent drain on the revenue, and are unjustifiable,
unless the advantage to the people from the construction of
the works be very great.   Yet, if cabinets are found willing
to incur them, and to face the discussion and publicity of effecting a loan for that purpose, how much more likely would
they be to do so if the proceeding required only a new issue
of notes ?

We conclude that the plan in question would not only encourage extravagance in the amount of the public expenditures, but would induce negligence as to the profitable investment of the capital for which the nation would incur obligations.

In general terms, moreover, we may say that as the Government is not in such immediate contact with the business of the country as bankers are, and would have no such delicate and instantaneous tests of over-issue as they have, it would be very apt, even with the best intentions, to cause frequent inflations. Of course they would be slight and short, but it is just as well to avoid them altogether.

The assumption by the government of increased power to issue Dominion notes—even though they were not made the sole currency—would also injure the business of the country. They would, in that case, have to monopolize certain new denomination— say " fours," " five," and " tens "—which would involve the restriction of bank issues to the same extent. The most obvious effects of this would be to limit the accommodation which banks could afford to their customers, and to prevent the mobilization of a large part of their assets in the form of currency. For the banks can now issue notes up to the amount of their paid-up capital, whereas they would then have to buy these notes, or make a large deposit with the government to obtain them. Either plan would tie up a part of their available capital, in the same way that the necessity of keeping a large reserve would, and with the same bad results. We know that elasticity is a prime requisite in a Canadian currency. It follows that any plan which restricts, or makes unprofitable, the required periodical issues is an injury, not to the banks alone but to the trade and prosperity of the country. It could only be justified if it were absolutely necessary, in order to secure the payment of the notes. Of course all the evils which would arise from the monopoly of the whole issue by the government would arise in some less degree from the monopoly of any considerable part of it.

On the whole, then, it hardly seems as if the advantages offered by a system of direct government issue beyond those of other systems counterbalance its especial failings.

In fact, it will be seen that all the systems spoken of

either have faults inherent in themselves or, though sound and safe, are unsuited to our circumstances. Is it not possible to combine the best features of two or more into a plan adapted to the needs of Canada? The task seems hopeful, and although the writer feels diffidence in passing from the discussion of facts and systems into the region of theory, he feels that it may be worth while to make some suggestions for the consideration of others with more technical knowledge.

The first requisite, of course, is absolute security; the second is such a measure of elasticity as will allow the public to get all the currency they require at any time; the third includes such arrangements as will provide a self-acting check on over-issue.

Our object then must be to choose some guarantee, which seems to furnish perfect security, and which may yet be consistent with elasticity of issue, and such a source and mode of issue as are least liable to cause inflation.

Perhaps we had best take the latter consideration first. We have already stated the objections to direct issue by the Government. We may recapitulate the advantages possessed by the banks as sources of issue. They have in their deposit account, and in the presentation of their notes for gold from time to time, a most accurate guage of the requirements of the public in the way of paper currency, and, since an excess of issue inflicts an immediate penalty, they have no temptation to do more than satisfy those requirements. Nothing but political motives could induce even a Government to do so, and banks are conducted on business principles alone. Of course one bank may, and does, strive to outrun another in competition for the supply of the existing demand. But none of them is anxious to force its notes on a market already known to be filled.

It seems then that banks are the best sources of issue. We may ask then what means shall we take to secure their notes?

It is clear that none of the plans which involve the covering of the whole issue, either by gold reserves or a deposit of bonds or other securities, can permit much elasticity. We are therefore reduced, by the terms of our problem, to the consideration of those under which only a portion of the note issue is so covered. It appears from our own experience that the reserves held by our banks are generally enough for ordinary transactions, though they do not provide for the case of insolvency. The banks are allowed to issue up to the amount of their paid up capital, and no moderate reserve would sustain the credit of such an issue, after the bank suspended payment. The holding of any reserve, much short of the entire circulation, must therefore be rejected on the ground of insecurity, or rather because it would not produce that public confidence which is as essential as the real and ultimate goodness of the notes.

But we have seen that the assets of our banks are quite sufficient when realized, making all allowance for losses in collection, to cover their note indebtedness several times over, and have considered whether making the notes a first lien on such assets would not be sufficient security. This we rejected, not because it would not provide for ultimate payment, but because we feared it might not prevent temporary depreciation during liquidation. Such a provision, if enforced in addition to the holding of a moderate reserve, would however give perfect security to any party who could afford to await the out-come of a liquidation.

Now the proposition the writer wishes to advance is this. Let the government compel all banks to hold a moderate reserve, take a first lien on all their assets, and then undertake to guarantee note holders against any loss by the failure of any bank. The most natural way of affording this guarantee would be for the government to print the notes, in the name of the different banks, and with a guarantee endorsed, and to issue them to the banks, within certain limits proportionate to the extent of their resources, as such bank might require them. The government would thus become responsible to all note holders to the full extent of the circulation, and it would have as security the reserves held by the banks to whatever extent might be agreed on, say one quarter of the issue, and a first lien on all the assets of the banks for the balance. Such a plan would certainly secure note holders perfectly, as the goodness of the notes would be affected in no way by the financial position of any bank. Consequently there would be no "run" of note holders on weak banks, and one of the chief causes of bankruptcy, and consequent loss by hurried liquidation, would be removed. When a bank was compelled, from ordinary causes, to suspend payment, the notes bearing its name would continue to pass current at their full value till such time as the assets could be realized. Then they would gradually be taken up, and their places would be supplied by new issues of other banks.

Whether it would be equally safe for the government would of course depend entirely on the details of the plan, and the care with which it was worked. If the banks were compelled to hold sufficient reserves, and if their financial soundness were carefully watched, and their supply of notes stopped when they grew weak, there is no reason to fear that the government would run any risks.

For instance, at present the total reported assets of the banks are in round numbers...	$176,756,000
Included in which are specie and Dominion Notes available as reserves,................	14,887,000
Their total note circulation is...	23,200,000
Balance of notes to be provided for out of general assets if they all stopped payment at this moment............................	$8,313,000
Balance of general assets....................	161,869,000

Or over $20 against $1 of notes.

The proportion in the case of individual banks may not be so favorable, but it is clear that Government would run no risk in assuming the note liabilities of our banks as a whole, if secured by a first lien on their assets.

It must not be forgotten that this plan would provide a source of revenue to the Government, which, if it entered into such a quasi-partnership with the banks, would claim a share of the profits derived from the issue of notes. The Bank of England pays the Government £200,000 a year for the right to issue £15,000,000 of uncovered notes, and makes another £100,000 of profit for itself. The profit would doubtless be greater here, and the proportion of its distribution would be matter for arrangement with the banks. Of course the latter would lose what they had to pay the Government. They would be partly recouped however, by the interest they would receive on the bonds which should form the greater part of their reserves. To most of them, also, the absolute immunity from runs of note-holders which they would possess and the consequent reduction of their gold reserves, would be nearly an equivalent for some loss of profits.

In any case, the interests of the public should have the preference over those of the banks in all new charters or renewals.

This plan seems to combine, in the greatest degree in which they are compatible with each other, security to noteholders, elasticity, automatic regulation of issues, and the division of profits between the banks and the Government.

The duty and position of governments in regard to paper currency are the same as in regard to coinage. Governments are the sole coiners, because they have special facilities for coinage and possess the confidence of the public. There is no other reason why they should be the only parties allowed to issue coin. If it were possible to exercise such strict supervision over private issues as would secure their genuineness, there is no reason why bankers or private parties should not make coin now as they did in ancient Rome. It is just as much the duty of governments to see that any paper currency which they make legal tender is genuine, as to prevent the counterfeiting of coin. We will go further and assert that it is their duty to see that all notes which they allow to be issued for use as currency are good. The taker of notes is in a different position from any other person who gives value for securities. He can form no opinion as to the value of the notes he accepts, unless from general report, or from consulting published returns not accessible to everybody. As a matter of fact he seldom thinks about the solvency of the banks whose notes he takes, until he hears some disturbing rumors. Many who take them suppose that all notes are money by the law of the land, and make no distinction between the "legal tenders" and bank notes that may be offered them in the same parcel. And there should be no such distinction. It is as disgraceful to a nation to have two kinds of paper circulating together, one of which is legal tender and the other is not, as to have two distinct coinages, only one of which is vouched for by the government.

Now, under the proposed plan or any similar one, all bank notes might be declared legal tender in all transactions, except for the redemption of other notes, as is done with the issues of the Bank of England. There can be no doubt that the possession of a currency whose goodness was unquestioned throughout the Dominion, and in foreign countries where the credit of the Dominion was good, would be one of the greatest possible boons to our trade and commerce.

FINIS.

www.ingramcontent.com/pod-product-compliance
Lightning Source LLC
Chambersburg PA
CBHW032358280326
41935CB00008B/615